COOKING WITH IRISH SPIRITS

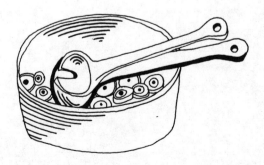

To John and Joanie and the Irish Spirit in us all.

Cooking With
IRISH SPIRITS

MARGARET JOHNSON

with illustrations by
Adrian McMurchie

Wolfhound Press

First published 1995 by
WOLFHOUND PRESS Ltd
68 Mountjoy Square
Dublin 1

ACKNOWLEDGEMENTS

I wish to express my thanks to the countless chefs, chef proprietors and Irish product
manufacturers who contributed recipes for this book, personally as well as by post,
phone, fax and photo. I would also like to acknowledge the cooperation and support
from the representatives of the Irish brewers and distillers with whom I have had the
pleasure of dealing while compiling these recipes: Oliver Dillon and Nancy Larkin
Rau, Bunratty Mead & Liqueur Co; Kevin Abrook, Grants of Ireland; John Clement
Walsh, Eily Kilgannon, Sheelagh Croskery and John Callely, Irish Distillers Limited;
John Harte, Cooley Distillery; Peter Walsh, Guinness Ireland; Mary Walsh, Murphy
Brewery Ireland; Thomas B. Halpin, E. Smithwick & Son; Siobhan Campion, R & J
Emmet & Company; Peter O'Connor, R & A Bailey & Co; John Keogh, Bulmers/Show-
erings, Ian O'Leary, Cider Industry Council, and Anne O'Curry's 'The Cider Industry
of Ireland'; Alayne M. Rooney, St. Brendan's Irish Cream Liqueur. Thanks to Carl
Hawker for his continuous computer wizardry; and my husband, Carl, who first and
always brings me back to Ireland.
Margaret Johnson

Ilustrations © 1995 Adrian McMurchie

The quotes in paragraph one and two of the Foreward are from the Time-Life book
Wines and Spirits, part of the series *Foods of the World*, 1968, Time Inc.; and Alexis
Lichine's *Encyclopedia of Wines and Spirits*, 1967, A. Knopf Inc.

British Library Cataloguing in Publication Data
A catalogue record for this book is available from the British Library

ISBN 0-86327-466-8
Cover photograph and design: Rai Uhlemann
Typesetting: Wolfhound Press
Printed by Redwood Books, Wiltshire, England.

CONTENTS

Foreword

Wine aficionado Alex Waugh, in his praise of grape and grain, suggests that 'man has been accorded by a kindly nature four stout companions to sustain and console him on his terrestrial pilgrimage: wine, spirits, fortified wines and beer.' These drinks, he feels, 'provide solace, relaxation and stimulus that a man needs if he is to complete with equanimity his arduous and often arid journey.' Consummate companions: perfect partners!

For centuries, the marriage of wine with food has been a happy one. Chefs, food writers and wine critics continue to extol the virtues of the two for the perfect partnership they create and for the ability to elevate ordinary recipes to extraordinary dishes with a mere splash of red or a dash of white. Wine-grower Alexis Lichine, in fact, calls the use of wine in cooking 'a positive pleasure. . .[in which] the two combine in a gastronomic treat infinitely more delicious than either could provide alone.'

In truth, wine is not used in cooking for its alcoholic content, but as a seasoning that enhances the natural flavors of foods with a mere suggestion of its presence. Through the years, imaginative cooks have learned to baste, marinate, tenderize, flambé, and deglaze with wine in recipes ranging from crêpes to chops, seafood to soups. But this book is not about wine—although James Joyce called Guinness 'the wine of Ireland' and Czar Peter the Great endorsed Irish whiskey with the acclamation 'of all wines, the Irish spirit is the best.' It is, instead, an attempt to form new alliances, create new marriages, and join the best of Irish spirits and brews with the best of Irish kitchens. The idea of a cookbook based on such relationships seems to be a logical extension of Waugh's philosophy, as well as of my theory of strange notions concerning Irish food and drink. Until recently Ireland was never associated with any kind of cuisine—boiled potatoes and Irish stew, yes, but never a cuisine. Dishes labelled 'traditional' usually included ingredients better left unknown—sheep's blood, mutton suet and pig's trotters among them—and not wholly realistic in modern Irish, American or European kitchens. Restaurants and hotel dining rooms were notorious for serving over-cooked vegetables and meats, with fish and pork somehow absent from most menus. No wonder visitors to

Ireland were unimpressed with what they were served.

On the other hand, everyone always associates Ireland with its national institution, the pub, and visitors forever extol the pleasures of 'sharing a jar,' 'pulling a pint,' or getting into the Irish spirit! With a reported 10,000 pubs in the Republic, another 2,000 in the North, and 1,000 in Dublin alone, no wonder visitors frequently number their fondest memories by the pubs they've visited. Indeed, the Irish pub is the centre of Irish life and the place where an estimated 2 million pints of stout are consumed daily!

By now, savvy travellers to Ireland have experienced the 'culinary revolution/gastronomic renaissance' that has been evolving over the past 15 years. Irish chefs have been steadily taking advantage of the country's natural bounty of produce, meat and fish on the way to developing a truly national cuisine. And what better way to accomplish this than to combine the pleasures of the pub with some creativity in the kitchen?

History tells us that in the absence of a wine-growing tradition beer becomes a nation's favorite drink. And like wine, which chefs have long known enhances the taste and flavor of food, Ireland's beer and ale, along with its whiskey, cider and mead, have been natural partners in many dishes, from plumping up the fruit in a Christmas pudding to tenderizing meat in a casserole or pie. With the addition of Irish cream liqueurs, spirit-flavored mustard, honey and marmalade, there seems to be no end to the ways in which Irish spirits and brews are creating culinary partnerships to complement centuries-old traditions.

Glaze a duck or baste a ham with Bunratty Meade or Irish Mist . . . make a stew with Guinness or Murphy's Stout or a soufflé with Smithwick's Ale . . . create a cake or sauté scallops with your favourite Irish Whiskey . . . braise pork or roast a lamb in Irish Cider . . . lace an apple flan with Irish Cream liqueur or a chocolate roulade with Irish Coffee Cream . . . dress vegetables with honeys flavored with Irish Mist . . . layer trifles with whiskey marmalade— the partnerships are endless. In fact, the 'wines of Ireland' that once held provenance in the pub are finding a new place in the kitchen, lending themselves to creations infinitely more delicious than anyone could have imagined.

I hope you'll enjoy serving some of the recipes offered here in the very first collection devoted exclusively to the marriage of food and wine, Irish-style.

Sláinte and *bon appétit*!

Chapter I
Whiskey With an 'E'

Most historians agree that the secret of distillation was brought to Ireland, probably from the Middle East, by missionary monks around the 6th century. They discovered the alembic the Arabs used for distilling perfume could be put to better use, and adapted it into a pot still. They found that if a mash of barley and water was fermented with yeast, then heated in a pot still, the alcohol in it could be separated and retained into a spirit with wondrous powers. They called it uisce beatha, Irish for 'water of life.'

When the soldiers of Henry II first visited Ireland in the 12th century, they were greatly impressed with this liquid (pronounced *isk'ke ba'ha*). They had difficulty pronouncing it, however, and eventually uisce came to be anglicized, first to fuisce, and finally to the word 'whiskey' we know today. The original official grant to distill whiskey in Ireland was issued in 1609 at Old Bushmills in County Antrim, but the distilling tradition on that site stretches back to as early as 1276.

For centuries, the fashion for Irish whiskey was widespread. Queen Elizabeth I was said to be very partial to it, almost certainly acquiring the taste from Sir Walter Raleigh who, by his own records, stopped off in County Cork on his way to Guyana to receive 'a supreme present of a 32-gallon cask of the Earl of Cork's home-distilled uisce beatha.'

In 1750, Dr Samuel Johnson defined it in glowing terms in his new Dictionary: 'Uisce Beatha (an Irish and Erse word which signifies the Water of Life). It is a compounded distilled spirit, being drawn on aromaticks; and the Irish sort is particulary distinguished for its pleasant and mild flavour. The Highland sort is somewhat hotter, and by corruption in Scottish they call it Whisky.'

Indeed, the difference between 'the Highland sort,' Scotch, and Irish whiskey is far greater than the spelling. While both spirits are based on barley, part of which is malted, the malt for Irish is dried in a closed kiln and not over open peat fires which give the smoky flavour that is typical of Scotch. That smoky flavour is deliberately absent from Irish, and some of the subtleties and delicacies of taste can be appreciated because of this absence. Triple distillation and a three-year maturing period are also uniquely Irish. It was these qualities that made Irish whiskey one of the favored drinks in both England and America at the turn of the century.

But the heyday of Irish whiskey production would not last forever. From the days when John Jameson founded his distillery in Bow Street in 1780, through the period of the political turmoil in Ireland (1916-1921) and Prohibition in America (1919-1933), the path did not always run smoothly. The distilling industry in Ireland withered for nearly four decades, until 1966 when the remaining whiskey distilleries joined forces to re-launch Irish whiskey in the world markets.

And for nearly two decades, Irish Distillers was alone in its production of brands like Jameson, John Power, Bushmills and Paddy. Expansion into the whiskey market occurred in the late 1980s when the Cooley Distillery of Dundalk, County Louth refurbished and reopened the old John Locke's Distillery in Kilbeggan, County Westmeath, installed a cooperage, and acquired the brand names of John Locke and Andrew A. Watt of Derry. Whiskey production resumed outside the realm of Irish Distillers, and the first mature cask of Locke's Irish Whiskey was tapped in 1992. The Tyrconnell Single Malt brand was relaunched the following year, and Kilbeggan, a well-known

19th century Irish brand, followed in 1994.

Whichever brand you might choose for drinking, you can be assured of a clean, smooth, mellow and smokeless taste. It's these same qualities that make Irish whiskey so appealing when used in cooking. The unique distillation recipe that produces the unmistakable, subtle taste of 'Irish' is responsible for an unparalleled array of flavours in foods from traditional to nouvelle. Simply put, a recipe built around a taste that took centuries to perfect is half-way there.

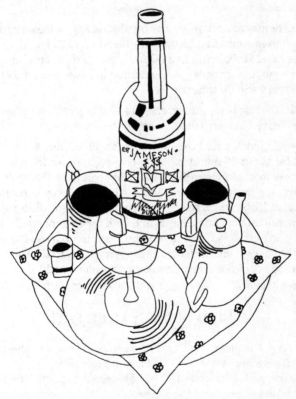

'Of all wines the Irish spirit is the best.'
Russian Czar, Peter the Great

CONAL O'SULLIVAN'S SEAFOOD ROULADE

1 egg	freshly ground pepper
2 teaspoons wine vinegar	*******
2 teaspoons dry mustard	4-6 crab claws
1 cup/250 ml/8 fl oz olive oil	1 quart/1 litre/1 ¾ pints court bouillon
*******	2 sprigs fresh fennel
6 tablespoons/90 ml/3 ½ fl oz good	2 tablespoons/30 ml/1 fl oz Jameson
quality olive oil	Irish Whiskey
2 tablespoons/30 ml/1fl oz raspberry	8 slices wild Irish smoked salmon
vinegar	3 cups/750 g/1 ½ lb mixed salad
½ teaspoon salt	greens

Prepare home-made mayonnaise by placing egg, wine vinegar and 1 teaspoon mustard in a blender jar. Blend on high for 30 seconds. Uncover and dribble in olive oil until the mixture emulsifies and thickens (about 1 minute). Add additional teaspoon of mustard to make it very stiff. Refrigerate.

To make the raspberry vinaigrette, in a shaker jar mix together olive oil, raspberry vinegar, salt and pepper (to taste).

Meanwhile, cook crab claws in court bouillon with the sprigs of fennel for about 20 minutes. When cooked, remove from bouillon and allow to cool thoroughly. Shell and then flake the claw meat. Mix with the mayonnaise and add the Irish Whiskey to dilute to a creamy consistency. Spread the crabmeat mixture onto slices of salmon, roll into cylinder shapes and chill for 15 minutes. To serve, arrange mixed salad greens on four service plates. Place two roulades on each and dress with raspberry vinaigrette. Serve with brown soda bread or toasted homemade white bread.

Serves 4 as a starter.   *from the Innishannon House Hotel, Co Cork*

MALTED WHISKEY LIVER PATE

½ cup/115 g/4 oz butter	1 tablespoon/15 ml/½ fl oz heavy
1 onion, finely chopped	(double) cream
1 garlic clove, peeled and crushed	2 tablespoons/30 ml/1 fl oz tomato
500 g/1 ½ chicken livers, well-trimmed	paste
salt and freshly ground pepper	¼ cup/60 ml/2 fl oz Tyrconnell Irish
	Whiskey
	chopped parsley (for garnish)

Melt the butter in sauté pan and cook the onions and garlic until soft and transparent. Do not brown. Add the chicken livers and cook for 5-7 minutes, keeping the centres pink. Remove from the heat and add the remaining ingredients. Put in a blender and process until mixture is smooth. Turn into a small mould or bowl, sprinkle with chopped parsley, and chill for several hours. Serve with water biscuits, toast or crackers.

Serves 8-10.

MEDALLIONS OF BEEF WITH BUSHMILLS

4 fillets (about 225 g/½ lb) of beef
2 tablespoons/30 g/1 oz butter
1 clove garlic, diced
1 teaspoon finely diced shallots
½ cup/115 g/4 oz mushrooms, chopped
1 teaspoon honey

½ teaspoon wholegrain mustard
2 tablespoons/30 ml/1 fl oz Bushmills Irish Whiskey
¾ cup/175 ml/6 fl oz oxtail-based stock
¾ cup/175 ml/6 fl oz heavy (double) cream
freshly ground black pepper

Sauté steaks in butter to desired degree. Remove and keep warm. Sweat off the shallots, garlic and mushrooms. Add honey and wholegrain mustard. Add the whiskey and flame. When flame dies out, add the stock and reduce by half. Add the cream and reduce slightly further. Adjust seasonings. To serve, slice fillets and pour sauce over.

Serves 4.   *from the Killarney Park Hotel, Co Kerry*

GRILLED STEAKS WITH BUSHMILLS SAUCE

4 sirloin steaks (about 350 g/¾ lb each)
salt and ground pepper
2 tablespoons/30 g/1 oz butter
4 tablepoons/60 g/2 oz shallots, finely diced

½ cup/125 ml/4 fl oz Bushmills Irish Whiskey
¼ cup/60 ml/2 fl oz tomato purée
1 ½ cups/350 ml/ 12 fl oz demi-glaze

Trim excess fat from steak and spinkle with salt and pepper. Place on an oiled barbecue grill and broil about 12 minutes until nicely crusted. Turn, season cooked side with additional salt and pepper, and broil to desired degree. Gently sweat shallots in the butter. Add Bushmills and reduce by half. Add tomato purée and mix well. Add demi-glaze and simmer for 10 minutes. Serve immediately with grilled steak.

Serves 4.   *from the Londerry Arms Hotel, Carnlough, Co Antrim*

The delightful flavour of Irish whiskey in sauces for basting and flaming is not confined to beef alone. It combines beautifully with a variety of meats, poultry and fish, and transforms the simplest cut of meat into an elegant entrée. One of the special features of cooking with Irish Whiskey is the lyrical names that chefs use for their dishes. Who could resist Ham Rosnaree, Chicken Cashel Blue, or Cockles and Mussels Molly Malone?

HAM ROSNAREE

4 tablespoons/60g/2 oz butter
4 ready-to-serve ham steaks
½ cup/125 ml/4 fl oz Jameson Irish Whiskey
1 cooking apple, diced
2 tablespoons/30 ml/2 fl oz honey

¼ teaspoon dry mustard
1 teaspoon cornstarch
½ cup/125 ml/4 fl oz light (single) cream
1 egg yolk
2 cups/450 g/1 lb mashed potatoes

Melt butter in fry pan and sauté steaks. Pour in whiskey and ignite. When flame has died down, remove steaks, add apples and cook for 2-3 minutes. Combine honey, mustard, and corn starch and add to the frypan. Stir constantly until mixture thickens. Add cream. Return ham to the sauce. Beat egg yolk into the mashed potatoes. Pipe the potatoes around the edge of a serving dish and brown lightly under the grill/broiler. Place the ham steaks in the center of the potatoes, cover with sauce and serve immediately.
Serves 4.

DUCK WITH BLACKCURRANT SAUCE

2 tablespoons/30 ml/1 fl oz oil
4 medium potatoes, peeled and sliced very thin
****
½ cup/125 ml/4 fl oz Jameson Irish Whiskey
juice of 1 lemon
½ cup/115 g/4 oz butter

****
4 breasts of duck
****
¼ cup/60 ml/2 fl oz Jameson Irish Whiskey
½ cup/125 ml/5 fl oz poultry stock
2 cups/450 g/1 lb blackcurrants
fresh chervil or parsley (for garnish)

Evenly coat a small fry pan with half the cooking oil, turn heat to medium high and arrange the potatoes in circular fashion, overlapping slightly. Add remaining oil, cook until golden brown, then turn over and cook other side until nicely browned. Keep warm.

Heat a small pan, pour in whiskey and cook until reduced by half. Add lemon juice and 2 tablespoons/30 g/1 oz of the butter. Stir to blend and keep warm.

Preheat oven to 375° F/190° C/Gas Mark 5.

Add remaining butter to a sauté pan and pan fry the duck breasts 2-4 minutes. Remove to an ovenproof casserole, pour lemon/whiskey glaze over and roast for 8-10 minutes.

While duck is roasting, reheat the small pan, pour in the whiskey and cook until reduced slightly. Add stock, reduce further, and add half the blackcurrants. Cook for 5 minutes, liquidize, and pass through a fine sieve to remove seeds.

Divide the potatoes onto four plates, arrange duck breasts on top and pour whiskey/blackcurrant sauce next to potatoes. Garnish with remaining blackcurrants, fresh chervil or parsley. The chef suggests an accompaniment of blanched carrots and courgettes parisienned into small balls.

Serves 4.   *from the Hibernian Hotel, Dublin*

Cashel Blue Cheese is a soft, mild blue cheese with a distinctive flavour and texture. It is one of a growing number of Irish farmhouse cheeses that are showing up on cheeseboards and in recipes in fine hotels and restaurants throughout Ireland. Made by Jane and Louis Grubb, Beechmount, Fethard, Co. Tipperary, it's a lovely ingredient in this chicken dish.

CHICKEN CASHEL BLUE

4 boneless chicken breasts	2 tablespoons/30 ml/1 fl oz olive oil
½ cup/115 g/4 oz Cashel Blue Cheese	3 shallots, chopped
flour seasoned with garlic salt (for dredging chicken)	¾ cup/175 g/6 oz mushrooms, chopped
1 egg plus 1 tablespoon milk (for egg wash)	2 tablespoons/30 ml/1 fl oz Irish Whiskey
½ cup/115 g/4 oz fresh breadcrumbs	¼ cup/60 ml/2 fl oz light (single) cream
2 tablespoons/30 ml/1 fl oz cooking oil	fresh watercress (for garnish)

Preheat oven to 350° F/180° C/Gas Mark 4.

Make an incision in each chicken breast to form a pocket. Roll Cashel Blue cheese into four cylinder shapes and stuff each breast pocket. Dredge chicken in seasoned flour, dip in egg wash and coat with fresh breadcrumbs. Heat the cooking oil in a sauté pan over medium heat and gently brown the chicken, turning to cook evenly. Bake in a medium oven for an additional 10-20 minutes.

Meanwhile, lightly sauté the finely chopped shallots in the olive oil. Add mushrooms and whiskey and cook slightly. Remove from the heat, add the cream and blend. Transfer the sauce to a serving dish, place the chicken breasts in the sauce, and garnish with fresh watercress. Serve immediately.

Serves 4.   *from Bailey's of Cashel Restaruant, Co Tipperary*

CHICKEN CAMELOT

2 boneless chicken breasts
115g/4 oz smoked brown trout
8 button mushrooms, sliced
4 tablespoons/60 ml/2 fl oz Jameson
Irish Whiskey

1 cup/250 ml/8 fl oz chicken stock
2 tablespoons/30 ml/1 fl oz light
(single) cream
fresh chopped parsley (for garnish)
6 cherry tomatoes (for garnish)

Make an incision in each chicken breast to form a pocket. Stuff with the smoked brown trout. Put the chicken stock and mushrooms in a sauté pan on the top of the stove and gently place in the chicken breasts. Pour whiskey over and cover. Poach gently for 10-15 minutes over moderate heat.

Remove chicken to a warm platter and reduce poaching liquid by half. Add cream and further reduce to a coating consistency.

Carve chicken breasts to resemble a fan. Pour sauce onto 2 serving plates and arrange the chicken slices on top. Garnish with freshly chopped parsley and cherry tomatoes.

Serves 2.   *from the White House, Kinsale, Co Cork*

The Russell Room Restaurant in Dublin's Westbury Hotel, headed by Swiss-trained Executive Chef Patrick Brady, is the only Dublin hotel restaurant to garner such an honour. Dishes like Brady's Chicken Anna Livia account for such acclaim.

CHICKEN ANNA LIVIA

2 tablespoons/30 g/1 oz butter
2 tablespoons/30 ml/1 fl oz oil
2 boneless breasts of chicken
2 tablespoons/60 g/1 oz onions, chopped
¼ cup/60 g/2 oz mushrooms, sliced
½ cup/125 ml/4 fl oz Jameson Irish Whiskey
½ cup/125 g/4 oz cockles shelled

½ cup/125 g/4 oz mussels, shelled
2 tablespoons/60 g/1 oz finely chopped mixed herbs
½ cup/125 ml/4 fl oz light (single) cream
½ cup/125 ml/4 fl oz chicken stock
chopped fresh parsley
salt and freshly ground pepper

Heat the oil and butter together in a sauté pan. Lightly cook the chicken on both sides, but do not brown. Add the onions and mushrooms and continue to cook for 5 minutes. Add whiskey and flame. When flame dies out, add remaining ingredients. Cover and cook a further 5-10 minutes until chicken is tender.

Remove chicken to a warm plate, correct seasonings, and sprinkle with fresh parsley. Serve with a mixed green salad.
Serves 2.

PHEASANT WITH WHISKEY, APPLE AND GINGER

4 tablespoons/60 g/2 oz butter
4 tablespoons/60 ml/2 fl oz oil
4 pheasant breasts, halved and boned
2 onions, thinly sliced
4 eating apples, peeled, cored and thinly sliced

2 inches/5 cm root ginger, slivered
1 tablespoon/15 g/½ oz flour
2 cups/500 ml/1 pint chicken stock
salt and pepper
¼ cup/60 ml/2 fl oz Bushmills Irish Whiskey

Preheat oven to 350° F/180° C/Gas mark 4.

Heat butter and oil together in a large ovenproof casserole. Lightly brown the pheasant breasts on each side. Remove and keep warm.

Add onions to casserole and cook until transparent. Add apple slices and ginger and cook gently for 2-3 minutes. Stir in flour and cook a further 2 minutes. Gradually add the stock, stirring continuously until the sauce boils. Season to taste with salt and pepper.

Return pheasant breasts to casserole, cover and bake for 35-40 minutes. Just before serving, stir in the Bushmills.

Serves 4.   *from the Hillside Restaurant, Hillsborough, Co Down*

LAMB IN LOCKE'S

½ cup/125 ml/4 fl oz Locke's Irish Whiskey
¾ cup/175 ml/6 fl oz olive oil
1 clove garlic, chopped
1 small onion, chopped

¼ teaspoon each thyme, rosemary, salt, pepper, cayenne
1 piece ginger root, grated
6 lamb cutlets, chops or steaks

Combine all the ingredients except the lamb. Place cutlets in a shallow dish and pour the marinade over. Cover and refrigerate for 12 hours.

Remove cutlets from marinade and grill for 5 minutes on each side. Brush with marinade before and after turning. Serve immediately with baked or mashed potatoes.

Serves 6 (depending on lamb cut).

LOIN OF VENISON WITH BACON AND BUSHMILLS

6 juniper berries
2 whole cloves
¼ teaspoon dried thyme
½ teaspoon black peppercorns
½ teaspoon salt
500 g/1 ¼ lb venison loin, boned and trimmed

¼ cup/60 ml/2 fl oz Bushmills Irish Whiskey
12 slices smoked streaky bacon
1 cup/250 ml/8 fl oz brown stock
½ cup/125 ml/4 fl oz heavy (double) cream

Grind the spices in a mortar and pestle or small coffee grinder. Slice the venison loin into 12 evenly-sized medallions and place in a large dish. Sprinkle the meat with the spice mixture and drizzle with 2 tablespoons/30 ml/1 fl oz of the whiskey. Wrap each piece of meat with a slice of bacon and secure with a toothpick. For medium rare steaks, sauté the medallions over high heat in a lightly oiled pan for about 5 minutes. Pour the remaining whiskey into the pan and carefully flambé. Remove the meat and allow to rest in a warm place while finishing the sauce.

Add the brown stock and cream to the pan and boil over high heat until it reaches a sauce consistency. Place 2 pieces of the venison on serving plates, spoon the sauce over, and serve immediately. Roast celeriac and buttered spinach are the suggested accompaniments.

Serves 6. *from Roscoff's Restaurant, Belfast*

*C*hef/Proprietor Brian Sinclair of The Old Schoolhouse Restaurant and Wine Bar, Swords, County Dublin, feels that 'the peaty scent of Bushmills Malt, a 10 Year Old Single Malt Whiskey, combined with the sea fresh flavours of scallops, mussels and prawns provides a rich dish' and one that is most popular at his restaurant. The light, fresh taste of fish, in general, is exceptionally enhanced with the addition of even small amounts of Irish Whiskey.*

SCALLOPS, PRAWNS AND MUSSELS IN BUSHMILLS SINGLE MALT

8 whole scallops
1 cup/250 ml/8 fl oz dry white wine
½ cup/125 ml/4 fl oz Bushmills Single Malt Whiskey
2 tablespoons/30 ml/1 fl oz lemon juice
2 sprigs fresh tarragon
1 medium onion, finely chopped
1.8 kg/4 lb mussels, scrubbed and cleaned
175 g/ 6 oz cooked, peeled jumbo prawns

¼ cup/60 g/2 oz butter
¼ cup/60 g/2 oz flour
¼ cup/60 ml/2 fl oz heavy (double) cream
¼ cup/60 g/2 oz fresh white breadcrumbs
¼ cup/60 g/2 oz Gruyère cheese, grated
pinch cayenne pepper
salt and freshly ground pepper
lemon wedges (for garnish)

Poach the scallops in half the wine, half the whiskey, lemon juice, tarragon and onion until they are just opaque. Place the mussels in a pot with the rest of the wine, then cover and simmer for a few minutes until they open. Discard any which do not open. Strain the cooking liquid from the scallops and mussels and reserve. Arrange the scallops, mussels and prawns in a deep serving dish and keep in a warm place.

Make a roux with the butter and flour and then gradually pour in the scallop and mussel liquid, stirring until smooth. Stir in the cream and remaining whiskey. Season to taste and continue cooking until sauce is thick. Spoon the sauce over the fish and sprinkle the breadcrumbs, cheese and cayenne pepper on top. Brown lightly under the grill/broiler and serve garnished with a wedge of lemon.

Serves 4.

Terry McCoy, Chef/Proprietor of The Redbank Restaurant, Skerries, County Dublin, says, 'I wouldn't be allowed to use very expensive fish ingredients in my dishes because everyone in Skerries knows the price of fish. Instead, I try to blend expensive fish with cheaper ones to balance the budget and make seafood exciting. This dish is one that the famous lady Molly Malone would have approved of.' Her lovely statue, at the bottom of Grafton Street, is a present from Jury's Hotel Group to the people of Dublin.

COCKLES AND MUSSELS MOLLY MALONE

2 cloves garlic, minced	6-8 large prawns
1 small onion, finely chopped	1 small monkfish
½ cup/115 g/4 oz butter	1 cup/250 ml/8 fl oz light (single)
2 tablespoons/30 ml/2 fl oz Paddy	cream
Irish Whiskey plus a splash	2 sprigs carrageen moss*
12 cockles or clams	2 tablespoons/30 g/2 oz cold butter
12 mussels	(to thicken)

Place the garlic and onions in a stainless steel saucepan and sweat with 1 tablespoon/15 g/½ oz of the butter. Add 2 tablespoons/30 ml/1 fl oz whiskey and flame until the alcohol dies out. Add the cockles, mussels and prawns, cover the pot and simmer until the shellfish has just opened. Do not overcook, or the fish will become tough. Remove the meat from the shells as soon as they're cool enough to handle. Reserve some of the best shells for garnish. Strain the cooking juices into a separate pan.

In a hot sauté pan, melt a little more of the butter and cook the monkfish medallions until lightly browned. Add the other shellfish and turn over quickly. Add the splash of whiskey and flame until the alcohol dies out. Remove all the fish to a large platter and keep warm. Return the cooking juices and cream to the pan, add the carrageen moss, bring heat up to high, and quickly reduce the sauce. When sauce has reached a nice consistency, reduce the heat, add in the cold butter and swirl to blend. Pour sauce over the arranged fish and serve immediately.

Serves 4.

KILMORE KING SCALLOPS

4 frozen puffed pastry shells with lids
2 cups/500 ml/1 pint fish stock
2 cups/500 ml/1 pint light (single) cream
1 cup/250 g/8 oz butter

12-16 large scallops, sliced in half
½ cup/60 ml/2 fl oz Jameson Irish Whiskey
1 teaspoon fresh dill, chopped
salt and pepper to taste
1 sprig fennel (for garnish)

Prepare puffed pastry as directed. Combine fish stock, half the cream and 5 tablespoons of the butter in a medium saucepan and cook until reduced to a sauce consistency. Remove from heat and keep warm.

Melt the remaining butter. Add the scallops and cook for 1 minute on each side. Add the whiskey and flame. Add the remaining cream, fish sauce, salt, pepper and dill. Bring slowly to the boil. To serve, divide the scallops and spoon into the puffed pastry shells with the lids at an angle. Garnish with the sprigs of fennel.

Serves 4.   *from the Bon Appetit Restaurant, Malahide, Co Dublin*

FILLETS OF SOLE ATCHEM

¼ cup/60g/2 oz butter
¼ cup/60 g/2 oz flour
1 ¼ cup/300 ml/10 fl oz fish stock
salt and pepper
½ cup/124 ml/4 fl oz heavy (double) cream
2 egg yolks
450 g/1 lb Dover Sole on bone
½ cup/125 ml/4 fl oz fish stock

2 tablespoons/30 ml/2 fl oz white wine
6 large prawns
2 tablespoons/30 g/1 oz butter
4 button mushrooms, sliced
¼ teaspoon each chervil and parsley
½ cup/125 ml/4 fl oz Jameson Irish Whiskey
Duchess Potatoes (see recipe below)

Prepare fish velouté by combining the butter and flour in a small pan and cooking over low heat for 2-3 minutes. Gradually add in the fish stock, salt and pepper, and stir until thickened. Add the cream that has been blended with 2 egg yolks. Stir again but do not let boil.

Poach sole on the bone in fish stock and white wine for about 15 minutes, or until fish flakes when tried with a fork. Remove and place on a warm platter. Peel prawns and sauté in butter with the mushrooms, chervil and parsley for about 5 minutes, or until prawns turn pink. Add whiskey and flame.

Pipe a border of creamed Duchesse Potatoes around two serving plates. Place 1 fillet in the centre of each, spoon on the prawns/mushroom mixture, and place another fillet on top. Coat with 1 cup/250 ml/8 fl oz fish velouté and glaze under the grill/broiler.

Serves 2.   *from Fitzpatrick's Castle, Killiney, Co Dublin*

DUCHESSE POTATOES

450 g/1 lb potatoes, boiled and mashed
salt and pepper to taste

2 tablespoons/30 g/1 oz butter
1 egg yolk, beaten

Combine all ingredients until thoroughly mixed and smooth. Pipe potatoes around edge of serving plates and place under grill/broiler (as described above), or into mounds on a greased baking sheet and bake in a preheated oven at 400° F/200° C/Gas Mark 6 for 25 minutes or until golden brown.
Serves 2.

PRAWNS ADARE

450 g/1 lb linguine or angel hair pasta
1.4 kg/3 lb prawns, shelled
1 tablespoon/15 ml/½ fl oz oil
1 cucumber, skinned and finely diced
1 red pepper, skinned and finely diced
1 clove garlic, chopped
3 tablespoons/45 ml/1 ½ fl oz Irish Whiskey

2 tablespoons/30 ml/1 fl oz dry white wine
½ cup/125 ml/4 fl oz heavy (double)cream
salt and freshly ground pepper to taste
½ cup/125 ml/4 oz natural yogurt

Prepare pasta according to directions.

While pasta is cooking, sauté the prawns in oil until lightly coloured. Add the cucumber, peppers, garlic and sauté a further 5 minutes, or until tender. Flame with the whiskey and wine. When the flame dies, add the cream and season with pepper. At the last moment, add the yogurt, simmer for 3-5 minutes, or until thoroughly warmed. Serve immediately over pasta.

Serves 4.   *from Adare Manor, Adare, Co Limerick*

DESSERTS

*O*ne of the most well-known and popular of all the 'Irish' cakes is the Irish Whiskey Cake which has as many variations as it has cooks. Some recipes are traditionally used for Christmas cakes, but of course, they're delicious any time of year and the preparation time is not as lengthy as the number of ingredients might suggest.

A delicious version of Irish Whiskey Cake is one that is produced under the label of Katie's Cakes, and made by CISTI Gougane Barra in Ballingeary, County Cork. Joan Healy, who makes Katie's Cakes, says that an Irish Whiskey Cake, with a consistency more resembling a fruit cake, would traditionally be used for a wedding or Christmas cake:

'A traditional wedding cake would have three tiers of Whiskey Cake, the top tier being stored away and used for the Christening Cake for the first child. These cakes were often made using Poitín (illegal spirits), and many country women kept a bottle in the house especially for the Christmas Cake. My great grandmother owned the original Gougane Barra Hotel called Cronin's and she always made Whiskey Cake which was served to the English "gentry" with their afternoon tea. The recipe that my great grandmother used is the one I use and which is still available in the hotel today.'

This cake will keep for years if stored in an airtight container and it matures with the whiskey. If used for a tiered wedding cake, double or triple the recipe and vary the pan sizes.

KATIE'S IRISH WHISKEY CAKE

1 ½ cups/350 g/12 oz currants
1 cup/225 g/8 oz sultanas
½ cup/115 g/4 oz raisins
¼ cup/60 g/2 oz glacé cherries
¼ cup/60 g/2 oz mixed peel
⅓ cup/75 g/2 ½ oz chopped almonds
juice and rind of 1 lemon

1 ½ teaspoon mixed spice**(see footnote)
½ teaspoon nutmeg
1 cup/250 ml/8 fl oz Irish Whiskey
1 cup/225 g/8 oz butter
1 cup/225 g/8 oz soft brown sugar
5 large eggs
1 ⅓ cups/300g/10 ½ oz flour

The day before you make the cake, soak all the fruit, lemon, spices, cherries, peel, and nuts in half of the whiskey.

Preheat oven to 275° F/140° C/Gas Mark 1.

On the day you make the cake, cream the butter and sugar until light and fluffy. Add the eggs one at a time, beating each in thoroughly and adding a little of the sifted flour with every egg. Fold in the remaining flour and mix in the soaked fruit one-half at a time. Turn the batter into a prepared 9-inch round/22.5 cm or 8-inch /20 cm square tin. Bake for 2 hours, or until cake is firm to the touch. When the cake is cooled, pour remaining whiskey over the top and store for at least several weeks to allow cake to mature. *Serves 10-12.*

**Mixed spice is not usually available in the U.S., so it is wise to mix up a small batch and have it on hand for Irish baking. Grind together 1 tablespoon/ 15g/½ oz coriander seeds, 1 crushed 2-inch/5 cm cinnamon stick, 1 teaspoon whole cloves and 1 teaspoon allspice berries. Add 1 tablespoon/15 g/½ oz grated nutmeg and 2 teaspoons ground ginger and mix thoroughly. Store in an airtight container and keep in a cool place.

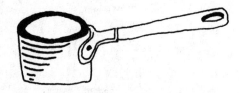

*A*n interesting 'boiled' version of this cake comes from The Hillside Restaurant, Hillsborough, County Down, and includes an exceptionally festive and rich addition of crushed pineapple and Old Bushmills Irish Whiskey. The cake is ideal for gift-giving when baked in small tins and also freezes well.

BOILED FRUITCAKE WITH BUSHMILLS

2 cups/500 ml/16 fl oz crushed pineapple
½ cup/115 g/4 oz butter
½ cup/115 g/4 oz brown sugar
1 cup/225 g/8 oz sultanas
½ cup/115 g/4 oz cherries
½ cup/115 g/4 oz mixed peel

1 teaspoon baking soda
½ cup/115 g/4 oz self-raising flour
½ cup/115 g/4 oz plain flour
2 beaten eggs
1 teaspoon mixed spice (see recipe above)
2 tablespoons/30 ml/1 fl oz Bushmills Irish Whiskey

Mix pineapple and its juice, butter, brown sugar and fruit in a medium saucepan and boil for about 5 minutes, stirring constantly. Remove from heat and cool completely.

Preheat oven to 325° F/170° C/Gas Mark 3.

Mix together flours, mixed spice and soda and stir in the beaten eggs. Add to fruit mixture and stir to blend thoroughly.

Bake in well-greased 8-inch/20 cm tin for 90 minutes. Test with a skewer after 1 hour. When cake is done, remove and set on a rack. Prick the top with the skewer and pour the Bushmills over while cake is still warm. Cool thoroughly, wrap in plastic wrap first, then in aluminium foil, and serve in a day or two (or freeze).

Serves 10-12.   *from the Hillside Restaurant, Hillsborough, Co Down*

KILBEGGAN RAISIN NUT CAKE

½ cup/115 g/4 oz butter
1 cup/225 g/8 oz granulated (caster) sugar
3 eggs
½ cup/115 g/4 oz flour, sifted
½ teaspoon baking powder
½ teaspoon nutmeg, grated
¼ teaspoon salt

¼ cup/60 ml/2 fl oz milk
⅓ cup/75 ml/2 ½ fl oz black molasses (treacle)
¼ teaspoon baking soda (bicarbonate)
2 cups/450 g/1 lb raisins
1 ¼ cup/300 g/10 oz pecans, chopped
¼ cup/60 ml/2 fl oz Kilbeggan Irish Whiskey

Preheat oven to 300° F/150° C/Gas Mark 2.

Cream together the butter and sugar, then beat in the eggs. Sift the flour with the baking powder, nutmeg and salt, and add to the eggs a tablespoon at a time, alternating with the milk. Mix together the molasses and soda and add to the batter along with remaining ingredients.

Pour into a greased and lined 8-inch/20 cm cake pan and bake for about 2 hours. Test with a skewer.
Serves 10.

IRISH WHISKEY TRIFLE

1 sponge cake, or package of sponge fingers
1 ½ cups/350 ml/12 oz can fruit cocktail, drained or
1 cup/225 g/8 oz fresh peaches, pears, bananas, strawberries
½ jar strawberry or raspberry preserves

½ cup/125 ml/4 fl oz Jameson Irish Whiskey
1 cup/250 ml/8 fl oz custard sauce (see below)
whipped cream
cocktail cherries

Split sponge cake into 1-inch/2.5 cm layers. Spread slices with preserves and put together again. Cut layers into small cubes and place in a glass bowl. Add fruit, sprinkle with Jameson. Pour custard sauce (see recipe below) over cake and chill. Before serving, decorate with whipped cream and cocktail cherries.
Serves 6.

Custard sauce, 'crème anglaise', or boiled custard, is a great beginning to a number of desserts. Flavoured with Irish whiskey instead of the more traditional sherry or brandy, it can be used with canned or cooked

fruit or over squares of plain cake. A jar of custard in the refrigerator is
perfect when you need a dessert in a hurry.

CUSTARD SAUCE

3 eggs or 6 yolks
¼ cup /60 g/2 oz white or brown sugar

⅛ teaspoon salt
2 cups/500 ml/16 fl oz scalded milk
Irish Whiskey to taste

Beat eggs or yolks together to blend evenly. Add remaining ingredients and cook over very low heat or in a double boiler over hot, but not boiling, water until the custard coats a spoon (about 6-8 minutes). Flavour with Irish Whiskey to taste. Chill.
Yield: 2 ½ cups/1 ¼ pints.

THREE LAYER CHOCOLATE MOUSSE

8 squares/225 g/8 oz unsweetened (dark) chocolate
½ cup/125 ml/4 fl oz heavy (double) cream
2 tablespoons/30 ml/1 fl oz Irish Whiskey
1 cup/225 g/8 oz white chocolate
2 tablespoons/30 ml/1 fl oz Baileys Irish Cream

8 squares/225 g/8 oz milk chocolate
1 ½ cups/350 ml/12 fl oz heavy (double) cream)
1 egg yolk
1 cup/250 ml/8 fl oz crème anglaise (see recipe above)
fresh strawberries (for garnish)

For the first layer, grate the dark chocolate into a small bowl. Heat half of the cream and pour it over the chocolate, stirring until it is completely melted. Add the whiskey. Whip remaining cream and fold into chocolate mix. Pour into base of a 2 lb loaf tin and allow to set.

For the second layer, grate the white chocolate. Heat the cream and pour it over the chocolate, stirring until it's completely melted. Add the Baileys. Whip the remaining cream and fold into the chocolate mix. Pour this over the dark chocolate layer and allow to set.

For the third layer, grate the milk chocolate. Heat ½ cup/125 ml/4 fl oz of the cream and pour it over the chocolate, stirring until it is completely melted. Add egg yolk and stir thoroughly. Whip remaining cream and fold in. Pour over the other chocolate layers, cover with plastic wrap and allow to set for one hour.

To serve, cut mousse into ½-inch /1 cm slices and serve on a bed of crème anglaise. Garnish with fresh strawberries.
Serves 12.   *from Echoes Restaurant, Cong, Co Mayo*

GAELIC TRUFFLES

1 ¼ cups/300 ml/¼ pint heavy (double) cream
8 squares/225 g/8 oz semi-sweet (plain) chocolate
¼ cup/60 ml/2 fl oz Irish Whiskey

⅓ cup/90 g/3 oz confectioners' (icing) sugar
1 teaspoon instant coffee
1 tablespoon/15 ml/½ fl oz hot water
½ cup/225 g/8 oz chocolate sprinkles (vermicelli)

Bring cream to a boil over moderate heat. Remove from heat, add chocolate and stir until chocolate melts and no lumps remain. Allow mixture to cool and add whiskey. Sift in sugar. Dissolve coffee in hot water and add to the mixture. Chill until mixture is firm enough to roll into small balls (1-2 hours).

Place chocolate sprinkles on a plate. Use two spoons or small ice cream scoop and form into walnut-sized balls. Roll in sprinkles to coat completely. Store in an airtight container and keep refrigerated. Use within a week.

Yield: about 24.   *from the Old Schoolhouse Restaurant, Comber, Co Down*

CHOCOLATE WHISKEY BONBONS

2 tablespoons/60 g/1 oz Dutch cocoa
1 cup/225 g/8 oz confectioners' (icing) sugar
½ cup/ 125 ml/4 fl oz Kilbeggan Irish Whiskey
3 tablespoons/45 ml/1 ½ fl oz light corn syrup

2 ½ cups/750 g/1 ½ lb vanilla wafers (digestive biscuits), finely crushed
1 cup/225 g/8 oz pecans, finely crushed
½ cup/115 g/4 oz confectioners' (icing) sugar (for dredging)

Sift cocoa and confectioners' sugar together in a large bowl. Mix the whiskey with the corn syrup and stir into the cocoa mixture. Add the crushed wafers and pecans. Mix thoroughly with a wooden spoon. Roll the mixture into balls about 1-inch/2.5 cm and dredge with confectioners' sugar.

Stored in a covered container, these bonbons will keep for a week or more, longer in the refrigerator. They're perfect for a dessert buffet and make lovely holiday gifts.

Yield: about 24.

*E*ven *breakfast foods can profit from a small addition of Irish Whiskey, especially Old Bushmills, a Northern Ireland favourite. Here are two unusual recipes, one for American style 'muffins with Irish flavour' from the Dufferin Arms, a traditional Irish pub/country restaurant in Killyleagh, County Down, on the shores of Strangford Lough; and for a tasty porridge from Grange Lodge, Dungannon, County Tyrone, 'guaranteed to help you face any frosty morning!'*

WHISKEY CLOVE MUFFINS

1 cup/225 g/8 oz white flour
1 cup/225 g/8 oz granulated (caster) sugar
½ teaspoon salt
2 teaspoons baking powder
½ teaspoon ground cloves

¾ cup/175 ml/6 fl oz milk
½ cup/115 g/4 oz butter, melted
2 eggs, beaten
¼ cup/60 ml/2 fl oz Bushmills Irish Whiskey
½ cup/115 g/4 oz walnuts, chopped

Preheat oven to 425° F/220° C/Gas Mark 7.

Sift dry ingredients together in a large bowl. Add milk, melted butter, eggs and whiskey and stir thoroughly. Add chopped nuts. Stir quickly and pour into large muffin tins lined with paper. Bake for 12-15 minutes, or until well risen and firm to the touch.
Yield: 12 muffins.

BUSHMILLS PORRIDGE

1 cup/225 g/8 oz oat flakes
3 cups/750 ml/1 ½ pints cold water
1 teaspoon salt

¼ cup/60 ml/2 fl oz Old Bushmills Irish Whiskey
brown sugar (to taste)
fresh cream (to taste)

Place oats, water and salt in a covered saucepan, bring to boil and simmer for 10 minutes. Divide cooked porridge into 4 pudding bowls. Pour 1 tablespoon/15 ml/½ fl oz whiskey around the edge of each bowl until the porridge almost floats, sprinkle with brown sugar and add fresh cream to taste. Serve immediately.
Serves 4.

POITÍN

The clear liquid known as poitín and pronounced *putcheen* is a drink of many names. Some call it 'The Connemara Doctor', 'Irish Moonshine', even 'Mountain Dew'. Poitín is actually a water-clear distillation of barley, sugar and pure mountain water. As in the production of whiskey, barley is steeped in water until it sprouts, then is dried. Later, this is boiled and distilled through what's known as a 'worm', a large spiraling coil. The manufacture of the fiery brew always takes place up in the hills close to the source of Ireland's crystal clear streams.

Its medicinal reference comes from the fact that poitín was frequently used as a cure for all sorts of ills; in fact, greyhounds are said to run faster when poitín is rubbed into their limbs, and horses jump higher hurdles when administered likewise. Some even claim that a fighting cock won the All Ireland Championship above the Cavan border in 1947 because his blood was fired with poitín! Poitín is also administered orally, the preference for most human consumption!

Despite its many admirable and medicinal qualities, its production in Ireland remains illegal, a fact that possibly contributes to the romance of drinking it. Illegal in Ireland, yes, but thanks to the determination of Oliver Dillon, who secured an export licence to distill poitín, it's now available everywhere except in the place where it was invented. Dillon's Bunratty Meade and Liquor Company, located at his Bunratty Winery behind the Castle in County Clare, is now the sole producer of legal poitín, but mind you, only legal away from Ireland.

Dillon calls his poitín Bunratty Irish Potcheen, and describes it as 'a truly spiritual thing that the Irish did long ago.' He credits the mountain men who distill the grain over peat fires as the 'real experts' in its production, but invites drinkers of his Bunratty Potcheen to 'taste and savour the bouquet of the mountain heather on the moonbeam edge that danced with Leprechauns in paradise, and recreate the Celtic magic that is Potcheen.' I don't think you'll be disappointed.

*T*his lobster dish is both delicious and traditional, a delightful combination but somewhat expensive. It should, therefore, be reserved for special occasions rather than everyday dining. For the best flavour, the fish must be freshly killed just before cooking. Do so by plunging a sharp knife into the cross on the back of the lobster's head. (Perhaps your fisherman will do this for you.) Slice the lobster in half lengthwise and crack open the claws. Remove all the flesh from the claws and tail and cut into large chunks. Keep both halves of the shell for service.

LOBSTER IN BUNRATTY POTCHEEN

½ cup/115 g/4 oz butter
1 live lobster , about 750 g/1 ½-2 lb
½ cup/125 ml/4 fl oz Bunratty
Potcheen

½ cup/125 ml/4 fl oz heavy (double)
cream
freshly ground black pepper
1 tablespoon /30 g/ ½ oz chopped
parsley

Heat the butter in a large skillet until foaming. Add the lobster meat and toss gently until the meat turns pink. Be careful not to burn the butter. Add the Potcheen and when it has heated up flame the pan. When the flame dies out, add the cream and heat through. Season with freshly ground black pepper and the chopped parsley. Pour into the reserved shells and serve immediately. A nice accompaniment is plain or parslied potatoes and fresh green beans. *Serves 2.*

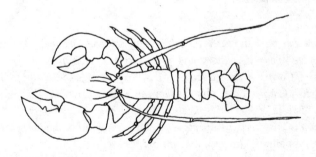

BUNRATTY POTCHEEN CHRISTMAS CAKE

2 cups/450 g/1lb mixed fruit
(sultanas, raisins, currants)
¼ cup/60 g/2 oz candied cherries,
chopped
½ cup/115 g/4 oz mixed peel
½ cup/125 ml/4 fl oz Bunratty
Potcheen
¾ cup/175 g/6 oz butter
2 tablespoons/30 ml/1 fl oz treacle

¼ cup/60 g/2 oz ground almonds
½ cup/115 g/4 oz mixed nuts,
chopped
1 ½ cups/350 g/12 oz self-raising flour
⅓ cup/75 g/2 ½ oz soft brown sugar
1 teaspoon mixed spice**
2 teaspoons almond extract (essence)
3 eggs, unbeaten
1 cup/250 ml/8 fl oz milk

On the day before you bake, place all the fruit in a bowl, pour Potcheen over and soak overnight.

Preheat oven to 325° F/170° C/Gas Mark 3.

Melt butter and treacle over gentle heat. Place all other dry ingredients in the bowl with the soaked fruit and mix well. Add nuts and spices and mix thoroughly. Add eggs one at a time and mix again. Add butter and treacle and stir again. Add milk. (Mixture should resemble a soft dropping consistency.) If too stiff, add either milk or another measure of Potcheen.

Grease and line a 9-inch/22.5 cm square tin and pour in the mixture. Leave a slight hollow in the centre. Bake slowly about 2-2 ½ hours. Test with skewer.

Serves 10-12.
** *See recipe on page 26.*

*Y*ou *can visit the three Irish Distillers' whiskey 'museums' to learn more about its history and production. In Dublin visit the Irish Whiskey Corner at the old Jameson Distillery, Bow Street, Smithfield; in Midleton, County Cork, tour the Jameson Whiskey Heritage Centre; and in the village of Bushmills, County Antrim be guided through the Old Bushmills Distillery. In Kilbeggan, County Westmeath, the Locke's Distillery Museum is also open to tours and tasting.*

To see how poitín is produced, legally, visit the Bunratty Winery, Bunratty, County Clare, behind the famous castle.

As well as gift shops, all the museums offer tastings at the end of the tour.

Chapter II
Affable Brews

The art of brewing was born possibly as long ago as 6,000 years. Some even suggest that it may have been a staple even before bread. Hieroglyphics have been found that seem to symbolize brewing, and some evidence of beer has been recorded in all languages. Next to water and wine, beer is possibly the most universal drink. In ancient times it was discovered that after harvesting sugar-rich ingredients like grapes, fruits, berries and honey, adding water and then leaving the mixture exposed to the warmth of airborne natural yeasts, a stimulating beverage would result. In those areas where starchy vegetation such as cereal grasses—wheat, barley, rye—were bred, the beverage came to be known as bouzah, after an old city in the Nile Delta, Bousiris.

The mystery of brewing eventually spread across Europe to the green and fertile land of Ireland where Neolithic inhabitants began to sow the seeds of an Irish brewing tradition by planting wheat and barley. From the 5th century, when St Patrick reportedly travelled around Ireland with his own brewer, a priest called Mescan, to the great St Brigid, who did the brewing for all the churches in the Kildare area, brewing was becoming an important art in medieval Ireland.

Enter Arthur Guinness, Kildare-born, who on the last day of 1759 would 'try his luck in Dublin' where he took a 9,000 year lease on a small, disused, ill-equipped brewery at St James's Gate and hoped to make it prosper. And prosper it did. After first brewing ale, Guinness found he would have to compete with a new drink, popular with the porters at Covent Garden and Billingsgate, which was being exported by London brewers to Dublin. Tackling the English brewers at their own game, Guinness tried his hand at the new 'Porter' and established a tradition that is, perhaps, unsurpassed in brewing history.

The characteristic dark colour of this new brew was the result of using roasted barley along with the the usual hops, yeast and water. Determined to brew a better porter than his competitors, in 1822 Guinness laid down exact regulations for the brewing of 'Extra Superior Porter'. The word 'stout', meaning 'hearty' and 'robust', was added in the early 1920s as an adjective describing porter, but the word evolved as a name in its own right. Today the world is blessed with having several Irish Stouts to choose from.

Murphy's Irish Stout, brewed at Lady's Well Brewery in Cork City, is the result of the 'energy and enterprise' of the four Murphy brothers — James, William, Jerome and Francis — who founded the family business in 1856. In the 19th century, Cork City was considered to be an excellent location for a brewery, close to the finest of malting barley from the country's limestone soils and the pure water of the River Kiln. This combination and location continue to be responsible for the creamy, mellow flavour of Murphy's Irish Stout.

Beamish & Crawford, another Cork Stout brewer, was founded by two local merchants in 1792 to compete with the increased importation of London Porters. Like other brewers who began with ale, William Beamish and William Crawford started brewing porter at Cramer's Lane in Cork, site of part of the present brewery, and have continued that tradition for two centuries.

The special association with Stout and food is a long-standing one, especially as an accompaniment to a Ploughman's Lunch, a platter of oysters, or a slab of beef. Guinness, in fact, calls this relationship 'The Perfect Partneship' and suggests that 'few things in life complement each other as smoothly.' I further suggest that Stout used in cooking is the perfect tenderizer for meat, perfect flavour enhancer for fish, perfect sweetener in cakes and pies. It is, shall I say, becoming a secret discovered.

GUINNESS

KIDNEYS ON TOAST

450 g/1 lb lamb kidneys
2 tablespoons/30 g/1 oz flour
pinch each salt and cayenne pepper
2 tablespoons/30 g/1 oz butter

1 ½ cups/350 ml/12 fl oz Guinness
¾ cup/175 ml/6 fl oz port wine
⅓ cup/75 ml/2 ½ fl oz brown stock
8-10 slices toast

Skin and dice the kidneys. Mix the flour, salt and cayenne together and dredge the kidneys in it. Melt the butter in an ovenproof casserole dish and cook the kidneys for 5-8 minutes or until golden brown. Add the Guinness and port and enough brown stock just to cover. Cook slowly with the lid off until the kidneys are tender and the liquid is reduced by half. Boil the kidneys briskly in the sauce until the cooking liquid is reduced to a glaze. Cut toast into triangles and evenly divide the kidneys over them.
Serves 4 as a starter.

AVOCADO WITH GUINNESS MAYONNAISE

⅔ cup/175 ml/5 fl oz mayonnaise
¼ cup/60 ml/2 fl oz heavy (double) cream, whipped

⅓ cup/75 ml/2 ½ fl oz Guinness
1 large avocado
2-4 leaves of crisp iceberg lettuce
2 sprigs fresh mint (for garnish)

Mix mayonnaise, whipped cream and Guinness together and refrigerate. Cut avocado in half, lengthwise, remove stone and peel. Arrange lettuce on 2 serving plates. Slice avocado from narrow end

to wide end, and fan the slices onto the lettuce. Spoon Guinness mayonnaise on each avocado and decorate with fresh mint sprigs.
Serves 2 as a starter.   *from the Ante Room Restaurant, Dublin*

TRADITIONAL IRISH STEW

½ cup/115 g/4 oz unsalted butter
1.4 kg/3 lb beef, cut into ½-inch /1cm cubes
3 onions, chopped
2 cloves garlic, chopped
1 cup/250 ml/8 fl oz beef stock

2 tablespoons/30 g/1 oz flour
1 tablespoon/15 g/½ oz brown sugar
1 ½ cups/350 ml/12 fl oz Guinness
1 tablespoon/15 ml/½ fl oz wine vinegar
2 bay leaves

Preheat oven to 350° F/180° C/Gas Mark 4.

Melt the butter in a heavy ovenproof casserole. Brown the beef a little at a time. Add the garlic and onions and brown gently. Add stock and bring to a boil. Stir in the flour and brown sugar. Add Guinness, vinegar and bay leaves. Cook in a moderate oven for about 2 hours or until the beef reaches a desired tenderness. Serve with boiled potatoes or white rice.
Serves 4-6.   *from Gallagher's Boxty House, Dublin*

FRANK SHEEDY'S MEDIEVAL STEW

2 tablespoons/30 ml/1 fl oz cooking oil
900 g/2 lb lean beef, diced
2-3 large onions, chopped
¼ cup/60 g/2 oz flour
6 carrots, sliced thick
1 head celery, sliced thick
2 quarts/2 litres strong beef stock

1 cup/250 ml/8 fl oz Guinness
1 teaspoon caraway seeds
1 tablespoon/15 g/½ oz raisins
1 tablespoon/15 ml/½ fl oz tomato purée
salt and freshly ground black pepper
2 tablespoons/30 g/1 oz chopped parsley

Heat the oil in a heavy skillet and brown the meat all at once over high heat stirring constantly. Cook for about 3 minutes. Remove the meat to a large kettle, reduce the heat, and cook the onions until soft, but not browned. Return the meat to the skillet, add the flour and cook with the onions a further 3 minutes. Transfer meat and onions to a large kettle and add remaining ingredients. Cook over low/medium heat on top of the stove for 2-2 ½ hours, or until meat is tender. Correct seasonings and sprinkle with chopped parsley. Serve with boiled potatoes or white rice.
Serves 4-6.   *from Sheedy's Spa View Hotel, Lisdoonvarna, Co Clare*

BRAISED BEEF WITH SEASONAL VEGETABLES

1 tablespoon/15 g/½ oz carrot, diced
1 tablespoon/ 15 g/½ oz onion, diced
1 tablespoon/15 g/½ oz celery, diced
2 tablespoons/30 g/1 oz butter
1.4 kg/3 lb topside of beef
2 tablespoons/30 ml/1 fl oz cooking oil
2 cups/500 ml/1 pint Guinness
6 cups/1.5 litre/1.5 quarts beef stock

bouquet garni
salt and freshly ground pepper
1 carrot
1 turnip
2 zucchini
1 bunch broccoli
¼ cup/60 g/ 2 oz cornstarch
fresh parsley (for garnish)

Preheat oven to 300° F/150° C/Gas Mark 2.

In a small sauté pan, gently cook the diced vegetables in butter. In a separate pan, brown the beef in hot oil. Remove the meat to an earthenware dish, add the stock, Guinness, bouquet garni and diced vegetables. Bring to the boil, cover and cook in the oven for 2 ½-3 hours.

Meanwhile, slice the carrots, zucchini and turnip into batons and cut the broccoli into florets. Blanch for a few minutes and refresh. When the beef is cooked, strain off the cooking liquor and thicken slightly with cornstarch.

To serve, thinly slice the beef and surround with the vegetables. Pour the sauce over and garnish with fresh parsley.

Serves 6. *from Acton's Hotel, Kinsale, Co Cork*

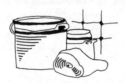

PIGEON BREAST IN MUSTARD SAUCE

4 pigeons
salt and pepper
2 teaspoons oil
2 tablespoons/30 g/1 oz unsalted butter
3 tablespoons/45 ml/1 ½ fl oz whole grain mustard

1 cup/250 ml/8 fl oz Guinness
¾ cup/175 ml/6 fl oz cream
1 tablespoon/15 ml/½ fl oz honey
1 tablespoon/15 g/½ oz butter
1 tablespoon/15 g/½ oz flour
fresh parsley (for garnish)

Preheat oven to 450° F/230° C/Gas Mark 8.

Lightly season the insides of the pigeons. Heat the oil in a roasting pan and add half the butter. Quickly sear the pigeons in the hot fat. Lay pigeons on their sides in a roasting pan and cook for 3 minutes, turn on other side and roast a further 3 minutes. Turn on their backs and cook a final 3 minutes. Allow to rest for 5 minutes.

Fillet the pigeon by inserting a sharp knife down either side of the breast bone. Slice very thinly, keeping a small piece uncut at the end of the slice so as to be able to 'fan out' the breast. (This will keep the pieces small and more tender.) Arrange the fanned breasts on 4 warm plates.

Meanwhile, pour the Guinness into a large pot. Bring to the boil, add the cream, mustard and honey and thicken with the roux of butter and flour. The sauce should be runny. Ladle over the pigeon breasts and garnish with fresh parsley.

Serves 4.   *from Oisin's Restaurant, Dublin*

DUCK IN GUINNESS AND HONEY

2 kg duck/4 ½ lb, trussed	1 cup/250 ml/8 fl oz Guinness
2 tablespoons/30 ml/1 fl oz oil	pinch each nutmeg and cinnamon
2 tablespoons/30 ml/1 fl oz honey	1 ¼ cups/300 ml/½ pint demiglaze or
1 tablespoon/15 g/½ oz brown sugar	duck stock
	pinch each salt and pepper

Preheat oven to 475° F/250° C/Gas Mark 9.

Wash and truss the duck. Brush with oil and seal in a hot oven until browned (about 10-12 minutes). Meanwhile, in a heavy saucepan mix together the honey, sugar, Guinness and spices and simmer for 10 minutes. Add demiglaze or stock and continue cooking for another 15 minutes. Season to taste with salt and pepper.

Reduce heat to 300° F/150° C/Gas Mark 2, cover the duck with the sauce and roast for 60-75 minutes. Baste occasionally. Test with a fork. If the sauce taste too bitter at the end of the cooking time, add a little more honey. Remove from the oven and allow to rest for a few minutes before carving.

Serves 4.   *from Dromoland Castle, Newmarket-on-Fergus, Co Clare*

GUINNESS BASTED ROAST LAMB

2 kg/ 4 ½ lb/ 1 leg lamb	¾ cup/ 175 ml/6 fl oz Guinness
1 clove garlic, cut into slivers	¾ cup/175 ml/6 fl oz Sherry
2 tablespoons/30 ml/1 fl oz olive oil	1 cup/250 ml/8 fl oz brown stock
salt and freshly ground pepper	

Preheat oven to 375° F/190° C/Gas Mark 5.

Cut the garlic into 8 slivers. Make incisions equally spaced over the lamb and insert the garlic. Brush the meat with olive oil, sprinkle with salt and pepper and set to roast in the hot oven (18-20 minutes per pound). Baste with the Guinness, a tablespoon at a time. Just before the lamb is finished, pour over the wine. Remove the meat, add stock to cooking liquor and skim off all the fat. Reduce the liquid by half, sieve, and serve separately in a sauce boat.
Serves 4.

SALMON STEAKS BAKED IN GUINNESS

4 fresh salmon steaks	salt and freshly ground pepper
4 slices fresh root ginger	¼ cup/60 ml/2 fl oz Guinness
4 tablespoons/60 g/2 oz butter	2 zucchini, chopped
1 tablespoon /15 g/½ oz fresh chives	4 tablespoons/60 ml/2 fl oz plain yogurt

Place the salmon steaks in an ovenproof casserole dish. Cover each with a few strips of ginger and a dot of butter. Sprinkle with the chives, salt and pepper. Add the Guinness and cover. Refrigerate for about 4 hours.

Preheat oven to 350°F/180°C/Gas Mark 4.

Bake salmon steaks for 15-20 minutes or until the flesh is pale pink and comes away easily from the centre bone. Lift out the steaks and remove the skin and bone. Place on a warmed serving dish and keep hot. Pour all the cooking liquid into a small pan with the zucchini and cook for 5 minutes. Remove from the heat, stir in the yogurt, and correct seasonings. Spoon the sauce over the salmon and serve with fresh new potatoes and broccoli.
Serves 4.

DESSERTS

*T*he Mills Inn, Ballyvourney, County Cork, is a colourful oasis in the heart of one Ireland's Gaeltacht areas. Ballyvourney is also the place of birth of my paternal great grandmother, Julia Crowley, so I find the location quite special. Mills Inn host Donal Scannell invites guests to 'enjoy one of the best pints of Guinness in one of the country's oldest pubs' (it dates to 1755), and when not pulling a pint for consumption, he adds Guinness to his pub's Porter Cake, another of Ireland's more famous desserts.

PORTER CAKE

2 cups/450 g/1 lb sultanas
½ cup/115 g/4 oz glacé cherries
½ cup/115g/4 oz mixed peel
1 cup/225 g/8 oz butter
1 cup /225 g/8 oz brown sugar
2 cups/450 g/1 lb flour

3 eggs, beaten
½ cup/125 ml/4 fl oz Guinness
½ teaspoon salt
1 teaspoon mixed spice**
grated rind of 1 lemon
¼ teaspoon baking soda

Preheat oven to 350° F/180° C/Gas Mark 4.

Put all the fruit in a large bowl and chop the peel. Cream the butter and sugar. Add the beaten eggs, one at a time, alternating with the flour after each addition. Add the Guinness and mix well. Add the salt, spices, lemon rind, fruit, soda and mix well.

Grease and line a 8-inch/20 cm baking pan. Pour in the batter and bake for about 2 hours. Allow to cool slightly before turning onto a wire rack.

Serves 8-10.

**See recipe on page 26.

APPLESAUCE SPICE CAKE

⅓ cup/75 g/2 ½ oz butter
½ cup/115 g/4 oz sugar
1 egg
½ teaspoon vanilla
¼ cup/60 g/2 oz seedless raisins, chopped
¼ cup/60 g/2 oz dates, chopped

¼ cup/60 g/2 oz walnuts, chopped
2 tablespooons/30 ml/1 fl oz Guinness
¾ cup/175 ml/6 fl oz applesauce
½ teaspoon baking powder
⅛ teaspoon ground cloves
¼ teaspoon ground cinnamon
½ cup/115 g/4 oz flour

Preheat oven to 350° F/180° C/Gas Mark 4.

Cream the butter with the sugar until the mixture is light and fluffy. Beat in the egg and vanilla. Stir in the raisins, dates and nuts. Mix the Guinness and applesauce. Sift the baking powder and spices into the flour thoroughly. Add to the creamed mixture alternately with the applesauce and beat until smooth.

Turn into a 8-inch/20 cm round tin which has been greased and lined with waxpaper. Level the top of the batter and bake for 50-60 minutes.

Allow cake to cook in its tin, but run a knife around the sides to loosen it. When fully cooled, cut it in half horizontally and fill and frost with lemon icing.
Serves 10-12.

LEMON ICING

½ cup/115 g/4 oz butter   1 cup/225 g/8 oz confectioners' sugar
juice and rind of lemon

Cream the butter and the grated rind of the lemon. Sift the sugar into the butter and beat until smooth and creamy. Stir in enough lemon juice to make the icing soft enough to spread easily. Fill the cake with about ⅓ of the icing and cover the top and sides with the rest. Smooth the surface with a spatula or knife blade dipped in warm water. Decorate with lemon and orange slice, if desired.

GUINNESS APPLE MINCEMEAT PIE

1 cup/225 g/8 oz beef suet
½ cup/115 g/4 oz mixed peel
juice and grated rind of 1 lemon
1 cup/225 g/8 oz currants
1 cup/225 g/8 oz sultanas
2 cups/450 g/1 lb raisins
1 teaspoon mixed spice**
½ cup/115 g/4 oz dark brown sugar

½ cup/125 ml/4 fl oz Guinness
2 medium apples, peeled, cored and stewed
2 cups/450 g/1 lb white flour
1 teaspoon salt
1 ½ cups/350 g/12 oz shortening
⅔ cup/150 ml/5 fl oz cold water
½ cup/115 g/4 oz chopped walnuts
1 egg, beaten

In a large bowl, mix together first 9 ingredients together thoroughly, cover and leave to mature overnight.

On the day of baking, stew the apples for 30 minutes. To make the pastry, combine flour and salt in medium bowl. Cut in the shortening using a pastry blender until all flour is mixed well to form small pieces. Sprinkle water over the flour mixture and toss lightly until the dough forms a ball. Divide the dough into two equal parts, wrap in waxed paper, and refrigerate for 30 minutes. Remove dough, flour on all sides, and roll out to fit two 9-inch/22.5 cm pie pans (top and bottom crusts).

Preheat oven to 350° F/180 ° C/Gas Mark 4.

Line the two pie pans with pastry. Sprinkle the bottom with ground nuts and build up alternate layers of sliced apples and mincemeat mixture. Cover with pastry lid and seal the edges. Make a few small slits in the crust to allow steam to escape. Glaze with a beaten egg and bake for 30-40 minutes.

Makes 2 pies; serves 8-10 per pie.

**See recipe on page 26.

GUINNESS CHRISTMAS PUDDING

½ cup/115 g/4 oz flour

1 cup/225 g/8 oz fresh bread crumbs

1 cup/225 g/8 oz soft brown sugar

1 cup/225 g/8 oz currants

1 ¼ cups/300 g/10 oz seeded raisins, chopped

1 cup/225 g/8 oz margarine, melted then cooled

1 teaspoon salt

1 teaspoon mixed spice**

grated rind of 1 lemon

1 tablespoon/15 ml/½ fl oz lemon juice

2 eggs, beaten

½ cup 125 ml/4 fl oz milk

1 cup/250 ml/8 fl oz Guinness

In a large bowl, mix together the first 9 ingredients. Stir in lemon juice, eggs, milk and Guinness. Mix well and spoon into two well-greased 1 cup/225 g/8 oz pudding tins. Tie pudding cloths

over or cover tightly with greased wax paper and aluminium foil. Leave overnight. Steam for about 7½ hours. If pudding is not going to be eaten immediately, cool, re-cover, and store in a cool place. At serving time, re-steam for 2-3 hours.
Serves 14-16.

**See recipe on page 26.

A lovely bread to enjoy anytime of the year, this recipe from Margaret Waterworth's Adelboden Country Lodge and Kitchen, Groomsport, County Down, has been specially adapted for this book from her commercially-made bread.

GUINNESS AND MALT WHEATEN BREAD

1 cup/225 g/8 oz coarse wholemeal flour	1 teaspoon salt
	¼ cup/60 g/4 oz butter
1 cup/225 g/8 oz fine wholemeal flour	1 teaspoon malt extract
½ cup/115 g/4 oz caster sugar	1 ¼ cups/300 ml/½ pint buttermilk
1 teaspoon baking soda	1 ¼ cups/300 ml/½ pint Guinness

Preheat oven to 425° F/220° C/Gas Mark 7.

Place all dry ingredients in a large mixing bowl. Blend in butter, lifting well to give air. Stir in malt, buttermilk and Guinness and mix to a porridge consistency. Do not overbeat.

Turn into a well-greased 8x8-inch/20cm square tin that has been sprinkled heavily with wholemeal flour. Sprinkle additional flour on top.

Bake for 30 minutes, then turn oven down to 400° F/200° C/Gas Mark 6 and bake a further 30 minutes. Cake is done when it springs back after gently pressing the top. Turn oven off and allow to cool with door open for 30 minutes. Turn out onto a wire rack. Can be eaten immediately.
Serves 10.

When in Ireland, visit the 'World of Guinness' exhibition in the Guinness Hop Store, Crane Street, Dublin 8. The Hop Store, originally built between 1876 and 1882, was sensitively restored to its original character in 1984, and now serves as a testament to the history of brewing. Antique brewing items, old wooden vats, even a reconstruction of a traditional floor maltings are part of the extensive touring area. Visitors are invited to sample the company's renowned product in a traditional Dublin pub setting at the close of their visit. The Hop Store also has a gift shop of Guinness-related items.

MURPHY'S IRISH STOUT

*A*s with any meat, long slow cooking in an Irish stout or porter develops its fine flavour. Beef cooked in Murphy's Irish Stout is no exception, in fact, beef casseroles or stews cooked in stout are improved in flavour if cooked a day in advance and reheated. Generally allow ¼-½ lb beef per person.

ELEANOR ARCHER'S IRISH STEW

450 g/1 lb stewing beef
2-3 carrots, thickly sliced
1 onion, roughly chopped
bouquet garni

salt and pepper to taste
2 cups/500 ml/1 pint Murphy's Irish Stout

Preheat oven to 350° F/180° C/Gas Mark 4.

In an ovenproof casserole dish, layer meat, vegetables and spices and pour Murphy's over. Bake for about 2 hours. Serve with boiled or mashed potatoes and a fresh green salad.
Serves 4.

BEEF AND MUSHROOM PIE

Double pastry crust
450 g/1 lb top round beef, cut into small cubes
1 tablespoon/15 g/½ oz flour
salt and freshly ground black pepper
¼ cup/60 ml/2 fl oz cooking oil
1 onion, chopped

1 cup/225 g/8 oz mushrooms, sliced
1 teaspoon Worcestershire Sauce
1 cup/250 ml/8 fl oz beef stock
¾ cup/175 ml/6 fl oz Murphy's Irish Stout
1 egg, beaten

Preheat oven to 350°F/180°C/Gas Mark 4.

Prepare double pastry crust (see page 43, in recipe for Guinness Apple Mincemeat Pie), or use frozen crusts and cook according to directions.

Dredge the meat lightly with flour and season with salt and pepper. Brown the meat in oil, a few pieces at a time. Remove and reserve. Add the onions and mushrooms and sauté for 5 minutes. Return the beef to the pan and add the Worcestershire, stock and Murphy's. Simmer over very low heat, uncovered, for 1 hour. If the mixture becomes too thick, cover halfway through.

Transfer the meat to a 9-inch/22.5 cm pastry-lined plate. Cover with top crust, crimp the edges, and brush with beaten egg. Cut slits into the centre of the crust and bake until golden brown, about 45 minutes.

Serves 8.

It's mussels, mussels, and more mussels at the annual Murphy's-sponsored 'Mussel Fair' held each May in Bantry, County Cork. Chairperson Eileen M. O'Shea likes this easy-to-prepare version of mussels steamed in stout.

BANTRY BAY MUSSELS IN MURPHY'S

3 kg/7 lb mussels
¼ cup/60 g/2 oz butter
2 large onions
1 cup/250 ml/8 fl oz Murphy's Stout

2 tablespoons/30 g/1 oz chopped parsley
salt and pepper

Clean the mussels well. Melt the butter in a large pan. Add the onions and cook for 2-3 minutes. Add the Murphy's and bring to the boil. Add the mussels, half the parsley, salt and pepper. Cover the pan with a lid and steam until mussels open, shaking the pan from time to time to distribute. Sprinkle with remaining parsley and serve with more melted butter.

Serves 4-6.

DESSERTS

W.D. Irwin & Sons Ltd, Bakers and Confectioners, Portadown, Craig-avon, Northern Ireland, commercially produce Murphy's Irish Stout Cake. They have provided this recipe especially for this cookbook for you to try at home.

MURPHY'S IRISH STOUT CAKE

1 ½ cups/400 g/12 oz raisins

1 ½ cups/400 g/12 oz currants

1 ½ cups/400 g/12 oz sultanas

½ cup /115 g/4 oz glacé cherries

½ cup /115 g/4 oz mixed peel

¼ cup/60 g/ 2 oz ground almonds

2 cups/450 g/1 lb flour

1 ½ cups/350 g/12 oz butter

1 ½ cups/350 g/12 oz brown sugar

2 teaspoons mixed spice**

1 teaspoon baking soda

grated rind of 1 lemon

4 eggs, beaten

2 cups/500 ml/1 pint Murphy's Irish Stout

Preheat oven to 300° F/150° C/Gas Mark 2.

In a large bowl, put all the fruit and nuts and mix together with a little of the flour to coat. In a separate bowl, rub butter into flour then mix together all dry ingredients except soda. Make a well in the centre.

Heat stout in a saucepan over medium heat, add soda, and while still frothing, pour into the center of the dry ingredients. Add well-beaten eggs and stir thoroughly for about 10 minutes.

Grease and flour a large deep pan or angel food tin and bake for about 4 ½ hours. Remove from heat and cool thoroughly. Wrap in aluminium foil and allow to mature for several weeks before using.

Serves 20.

** See recipe on page 26.

SMITHWICK'S ALE

While other Irish brewers eventually switched from ale to stout, John Smithwick, who founded Ireland's oldest brewery at St Francis Abbey, continued to brew ale using the finest of local resources. Ample supplies of soft water from the nearby Nore and Breagagh Rivers, locally grown barley and hops, and the best available strains of yeast continue to be the only ingredients in Smithwick's Ale.

John Smithwick first began brewing in 1710 at the site of the 14th century Abbey of St Francis in the heart of the medieval city of Kilkenny. While at least eight families in Kilkenny were engaged in the business of common or public brewing at this time, it was the Smithwick Brewery that prospered and grew, especially during the lifetime of Edmund Smithwick (1800-1876), for whom the current brewery, E. Smithwick's & Sons, Ltd, is named.

The golden colour, rich and satisfying flavour offer a delightful alternative to those who prefer drinking ale over Stout. These same qualities make it an exceptional choice in cooking. The light, delicate flavour of Smithwick's Ale is perfect for making batters for frying vegetables and seafood, and is an excellent source of liquid in the making of special cakes and puddings.

Thomas B. Halpin, affable and knowledgable retired Brewing and Food Science Consultant for E. Smithwick & Sons Ltd, suggested to me that when using beers and ales in cooking they should be de-gassed first. Since all beers contain up to 5 grams of CO^2 per litre, he suggests decantation from one container to another, about six times, in order to remove some of the gas.

*C*hefs *from Parliament House Restaurant in Kilkenny, situated directly across from the entrance to St Francis Abbey Brewery, and from Acton's Hotel in Kinsale both offered this recipe for Mushrooms in Ale Batter, the first suggesting an accompaniment of Garlic Mayonnaise, the other Tarragon Mayonnaise. Both are perfect for starters. You make the choice!*

MUSHROOMS IN ALE BATTER

1 ¾ cups/350 g/12 oz flour
1 ½ teaspoons salt
1 tablespoon/30 g/½ oz sugar
4 eggs
2 cups/500 ml/1 pint Smithwick's Ale
⅓ cup/75 ml/2 ½ fl oz cooking oil
24 large fresh mushrooms
oil for frying

****
½ cup/125 ml/4 fl oz homemade mayonnaise
1-2 cloves garlic, minced
****
½ cup/125 ml/4 fl oz homemade mayonnaise
3 leaves fresh tarragon, chopped

Sift flour , salt and sugar into a large bowl and make a well. Break eggs into the centre, mix in Smithwick's and oil. Gradually mix together with the flour and whisk to a smooth batter. Dip mushrooms in batter and cook in hot oil until golden brown.

Meanwhile, prepare homemade mayonnaise according to directions on page 109 and mix with either garlic or tarragon.
Serves 4 as a starter.

FRIED SHRIMP IN SMITHWICK'S

450 g/1 lb raw shrimp, shelled and deveined
1 tablespoon/15 ml/½ fl oz lemon juice
½ teaspoon Worcestershire Sauce
½ cup/115 g/4 oz flour
pinch salt

1 tablespoon/15 g/1 ½ oz butter, melted
1 egg, beaten
½ cup/125 ml/4 fl oz Smithwick's
1 egg white, stiffly beaten
oil for frying

Marinate the shrimp in the lemon juice and Worcestershire sauce for about 15 minutes.

Prepare the batter by sifting the flour and salt into a mixing bowl. Stir in the butter and egg. Add the Smithwick's gradually, stirring only until the mixture is smooth. Allow the batter to rest in a warm place for an hour, then fold in the beaten egg white.

Dip a few shrimp at a time in the batter and fry in deep hot oil until golden brown. Drain on absorbent paper. Serve with Garlic or Tarragon Mayonnaise (recipes above) or Honey Mustard Sauce (see below).

Serves 4 as a starter.

HONEY MUSTARD SAUCE

½ cup/125 ml/4 fl oz mayonnaise
2 tablespoons/30 ml/1 fl oz Dijon mustard

2 tablespoons/30 ml/1 fl oz honey
1 teaspoon white vinegar
1 teaspoon white pepper

Whisk all ingredients together in a small bowl. Allow to stand at room temperature for about 10 minutes before serving.

SMITHWICK'S CHEESE SOUFFLE

2 tablespoons/30 g/1 oz butter
3 tablespoons/45 g/ 1 ½ oz flour
1 cup/250 ml/8 fl oz Smithwick's
6 eggs, separated
½ cup/115 g/4 oz Swiss Cheese, shredded

¼ cup/60 g/2 oz Parmesan Cheese, grated
dash cayenne pepper
½ teaspoon nutmeg
½ teaspoon salt
⅛ teaspoon cream of tartar

Preheat oven to 375° F/190 ° C/Gas Mark 5.

Line a soufflé dish with greased waxed paper, making sure the paper extends a few inches over the top of the dish. Melt the butter in a small saucepan, add the flour, and cook together for about 1 minute. Stir in the Smithwick's gradually and whisk to form a medium sauce. Add 4 egg yolks, then the grated and shredded cheeses, pepper and nutmeg. Mix thoroughly.

Beat 6 egg whites with salt and cream of tartar until they form stiff peaks. Stir 1 cup of the whites into the cheese, then gently fold in remainder. Pour into soufflé dish and bake for 25 minutes.

Serves 4.

BAKED HAM IN SMITHWICK'S

¾ cup/175 g/6 oz raisins
warm water
6kg/12-13 lb precooked ham
20 whole cloves
2 teaspoons dry mustard
½ cup/125 ml/4 fl oz molasses
(treacle)

2 cups/500 ml/1 pint Smithwick's
2 ½ tablespoons/45 g/1 ½ oz
cornstarch
⅓ cup/75 ml/2 ½ fl oz water
2 tablespoons/30 ml/1 fl oz wine
vinegar

Preheat oven to 325°F/170°C/Gas Mark 3.

Cover the raisins with warm water. Stud the ham with cloves. Mix together the mustard and molasses and spread evenly over the ham. Bake 1 hour, basting with the Smithwick's.

When the ham is cooked, transfer to a warm platter. Put the roasting pan on top of the stove and, over medium heat, reduce the pan drippings to 1 ½ cups/350 ml/12 fl oz. Drain the water from the raisins into a measuring cup and add enough water to make 1 cup/250 ml/8 fl oz. Add to the drippings and bring to the boil. Mix the cornstarch with the water, add to the broth and boil, stirring continuously, for 1 minute. Add the vinegar and raisins. Serve the sauce in a gravy boat with the sliced ham. If desired, accompany further with Red Cabbage and Smithwick's, page 53.
Serves 10-12 generously.

POT ROAST IN SMITHWICK'S

4 slices bacon
1.8 kg/4 lb pot roast
1 ½ cups/350 ml/12 fl oz Smithwick's
1 cup/250 ml/8 fl oz beef stock
1 tablespoon/15 ml/½ fl oz wine
vinegar
2 tablespoons/60 g/1 oz sugar
1-2 cloves garlic

1 tablespoon/30 g/½ oz salt
1 tablespoon/30 g/½ oz thyme
6 each whole cloves and peppercorns,
crushed
dash cayenne pepper
6 baking potatoes
12 pearl onions
2 carrots, sliced thick

Preheat oven to 350° F/180° C/Gas Mark 4.

Sauté the bacon until crisp, then remove to absorbent paper. When well-drained, crumble bacon into an ovenproof casserole dish. Brown the pot roast in the bacon fat then place the beef over the crumbled bacon. Mix together remaining 9 ingredients and pour over the beef. Bake for about 2 hours. After 1 hour, put 6 baking potatoes in the oven to accompany the meat, and add the onions

and carrots to the pot roast. At the end of the cooking time, remove meat from pan and keep warm. Pour pan juices into a small saucepan and thicken with a little roux. Slice beef onto serving plates, add baked potato and divide onions and carrots equally. Serve gravy in a sauce boat.
Serves 6.

RED CABBAGE WITH SMITHWICK'S

10 slices bacon
2 onions, chopped
2 green apples, peeled, cored and sliced
1 small head red cabbage, shredded

1 tablespoon/15 ml/ ½ fl oz red currant jelly
pinch nutmeg
½ cup/125 ml/4 fl oz Smithwick's
salt and freshly fround black pepper
1 teaspoon caraway seeds

Preheat oven to 375° F/190° C/Gas Mark 5.

In a large sauté pan, fry the bacon until crisp, then remove to absorbent paper. Sauté onions and apples in the bacon drippings. Transfer to a deep ovenproof casserole dish, add remaining ingredients along with the crumbled bacon, and stir to blend. Cover and bake for 40 minutes.
Serves 4.

DESSERTS

RASPBERRY SOUFFLE

½ cup/125 ml/4 fl oz Smithwick's
3 tablespoons/45 g/1 ½ oz butter
2 tablespoons/60 g/1 oz raspberries
¼ cup/60 g/2 oz sugar
3 eggs separated

2 tablespoons/60 g/1 oz flour
1 tablespoon/15 g/½ oz butter
1 tablespoon/15 g/½ oz sugar
2 tablespoons/60 g/1 oz confectioners' (icing) sugar

Preheat oven to 400° F/200° C/Gas Mark 6.

Place the Smithwick's in a small saucepan and bring to a boil. In a small mixing bowl, cream the butter to a smooth paste. Add the hot ale slowly, whisking in well. Return the mixture to the pan and boil again, stirring constantly. Cool gently for 2-3 minutes. Remove from stove and allow to cool further. Add raspberries, sugar and 3 egg yolks to mixture and blend.

Grease and dust with sugar a 6-inch/15 cm soufflé mould. In a clean bowl, whisk egg whites to form stiff peaks. Add quarter to the Smithwick's mixture, then gently fold in remaining whites. Pour into soufflé mould and bake for 20-25 minutes. Sprinkle with confectioners' sugar and cook further for 5 minutes to glaze. Serve immediately.

Serves 4.   *from the Parliament House Restaurant, Kilkenny*

KITTY STALLARD'S ALE GATEAU

¾ cup/175 g/6 oz flour

pinch of salt

2 teaspoons baking powder

½ teaspoon ginger

⅔ cup/150 ml/5 fl oz Smithwick's

2 eggs, separated

½ cup/115 g/4 oz brown sugar

⅓ cup/75 ml/2 ½ fl oz corn oil

1 teaspoon white sugar (for egg whites)

¼ cup/60 g/2 oz white sugar

⅓ cup/75 ml/2 ½ fl oz Smithwick's

1 cup/250 ml/8 fl oz cream

¼ cup/60 g/2 oz grated chocolate

Preheat oven to 325° F/170° C/Gas Mark 3.

Sift flour, salt, baking powder and ginger into a bowl. Make a well in the centre and add half the Smithwick's, egg yolks, brown sugar and corn oil. Beat well. Beat the egg whites until stiff, mix in the white sugar and fold into the mixture. Grease and flour an 8-inch/20 cm baking tin. Gently pour in the batter and bake for about 30 minutes. Cool on a wire rack.

For the syrup, warm the remaining ale and dissolve the sugar in it. Turn the cake upside down and pour the syrup over it. Leave overnight. Just before serving, whip the cream and cover the cake. Sprinkle the grated chocolate over it.

Serves 8-10.

Chapter III
Of Heather and Honey

Of all the world's liquors, wine is the oldest. Archaeologists maintain that grape wine, in fact, was made at least 10,000 years ago, with mention of wine as 'a gift from the gods' found in Egyptian, Greek and Roman history. Ancient scholars tell of Noah's planting a vineyard near Erivan, and the Old Testament mentions wine more than 150 times. Since grape seeds have been found in prehistoric caves, it is conceivable that grape wine is older than history.

But even before the advent of grape wine, honey was fermented with water and herbs to create a liquor known as mead. This honey-based wine came to Britain and Ireland in the 5th century as the drink of the Anglo, Saxon and Jute warriors, although it was already being produced by secretive Irish monks who fermented their excess honey with water, grape juice and herbs. Mead came to be the chief drink of the Irish and is often mentioned in Gaelic poetry. Its influence was so great that the Halls of Tara, where the High Kings of Ireland ruled, was called the House of the Mead Circle. Its fame as a refreshing drink spread quickly throughout Ireland, and soon no medieval banquet was complete without mead to accompany it.

This honey-wine was also believed to have powers of virility and fertility, and it became the custom at weddings for the bride and groom to be toasted with special goblets full of mead which they would use for one full moon after the wedding. This tradition is the origin of the word 'honeymoon'.

But with the tumult of the Middle Ages, the monks' secret method of making mead was lost to the Irish for over 500 years. It wasn't until recently that the recipe for mead was redis-covered. Today, mead is once again being produced in Ireland by Oliver Dillon at his Bunratty Winery, an old coach house

situated in the shadow of the now-famous Bunratty Castle in County Clare. This ancient drink, always regarded as one 'fit for a king', has been reinvented for the modern world to be drunk as an aperitif or table wine. It is also the mainstay at Ireland's popular medieval castle banquets.

Bunratty Meade is equally pleasant as an ingredient in cook-ing. Its mellow taste adds a subtle sweetness to meats, poultry and vegetables, and like other fine wines used in cooking, it can be the basis of an exciting and elegant meal, one even 'fit for a king'.

Like mead, heather wine, a spirit with overtones of honey, herbs and spices, had been a favourite of the chieftains and nobles of Ireland's ancient clans. The secret of this legendary drink also disappeared for centuries with the great exodus of the Irish Earls in 1691, an event which has passed into Irish history as 'The Flight of the Wild Geese'.

The recipe was thought to be lost forever until some Euro-pean travellers visiting Ireland in the 1940s produced an old manuscript they had found. Daniel E. Williams, whose family founded the Tullamore Distillery, recognized it as the ancient recipe for heather wine and transformed it into what is now Irish Mist Liqueur.

Inherent in the transformation was Williams' devotion to the authenticity and originality of Ireland's legendary liqueur—the blending of four great distilled spirits, the mellowing and maturing process, the mingling of Irish honeys and exotic herbs. Yet as treasured and exceptional as Irish Mist is, it remains a drink for all occasions—neat, with ice or soda. Its perfect balance of potency, good taste and bouquet makes it an extraordinary ingredient in food as well, complementing meats and fish and adding incomparable flavour to desserts. The natural taste of mead, rediscovered in drink, is making its presence known in the kitchen as well.

BUNRATTY MEADE

CHICKEN CUCHULAIN

1 cup/225 g/8 oz mushrooms, sliced
1 onion, chopped
2 tablespoons/30 g/1 oz butter
¼ cup/60 g/2 oz flour
1 ½ cups/350 ml/12 fl oz milk
 salt and white pepper to taste

¼ cup /60 g/2 oz chopped parsley
¼ cup/60 g/2 oz chopped pimento
2 cups/450 g/1 lb cooked chicken, diced
¾ cup/175 ml/6 fl oz Bunratty Meade
buttered toast, white rice or thin egg noodles

Sauté mushrooms and onion in butter for about 10 minutes. Blend in flour, then add milk slowly, stirring constantly until thickened. Season to taste with salt and pepper. Add parsley, pimento and chicken pieces and cook slowly, covered, for 15 minutes. Stir in Bunratty Meade and heat further for 5 minutes. Served on hot buttered toast, white rice, or thin egg noodles.
Serves 4 as a starter.

EARL OF THOMOND POULET

6 boneless chicken breasts
½ cup/115 g/4 oz flour
⅓ cup/75 g/2 ½ oz unsalted butter
salt and pepper to taste
⅓ cup/75 ml/2 fl oz Bunratty Meade
½ cup/125 ml/4 fl oz cider

½ cup/125 ml/4 fl oz heavy (double)cream
6 apples, peeled, cored and sliced
4 tablespoons/60 g/2 oz unsalted butter
2 tablespoons/30 g/1 oz sugar
watercress (for garnish)

Dredge the chicken breasts in flour. Melt the butter in a heavy skillet, add the chicken and cook 4-5 minutes on each side over medium heat. Do not brown. Sprinkle with salt and pepper. Remove the chicken breasts to a serving platter and keep warm.

Heat the Bunratty Meade in a small saucepan. Add cider and cream and continue to cook further for 5-6 minutes. Reserve the sauce.

Sauté the sliced apples in the butter, sprinkle with sugar, and cook until the edges are slightly crisp.

To serve, arrange the chicken breasts on plates, spoon a little sauce over each of the breasts, arrange the apple slices around the chicken and garnish with fresh sprigs of watercress.
Serves 6.

CRAGGAUNOWEN CHICKEN

6 boneless chicken breasts
½ cup/115 g/4 oz mushrooms, finely chopped
½ cup/115 g/4 oz fresh white bread crumbs
½ teaspoon tarragon
3 tablespoons/45 g/1 ½ oz parsley
⅓ cup/75 g/2 ½ oz golden raisins, finely chopped

⅓ cup/75 g/2 ½ oz walnuts, finely chopped
⅓ cup/75 g/2 ½ oz apples, finely chopped
salt and freshly ground black pepper
1 cup/250 ml/8 fl oz Bunratty Meade
6 tablespoons/90 g/3 oz unsalted butter, melted
1 cup/250 ml/8 fl oz chicken stock
fresh parsley (for garnish)

Preheat oven to 350°F/180°C/Gas Mark 4.

Place the chicken breasts between two sheets of waxed paper and pound thin. In a mixing bowl combine the next 8 ingredients. Moisten with half of the Bunratty Meade and half of the melted butter. If necessary, add more butter to make the stuffing sufficiently moist.

Lay out the chicken breasts and brush one side with melted butter. Season with salt and pepper. Place 1 spoon of stuffing in the centre of each breast. Fold in each of the sides, envelope-style, and place seam side down on an greased ovenproof casserole dish. Brush again with remaining melted butter and bake for 25 minutes, basting frequently with the pan juices. Mix remaining Bunratty Meade with chicken stock and pour over the chicken. Cook further for 25 minutes and continue to baste. Garnish with parsley.
Serves 6.

KING JOHN'S PEPPERED STEAK

2 tablespoons/30 g/1 oz freshly
ground black pepper
6 club steaks (about 175g /6oz)
6 tablespoons/90 g/3 oz butter
1 tablespoon/15ml/½ fl oz
Worcestershire Sauce

1 tablespoon/15ml/½ fl oz lemon juice
1 teaspoon Tabasco Sauce
4 tablespoons/60 ml/2 fl oz Bunratty
Meade
1 tablespoon/15 g/½ oz each parsley
and chives

Press pepper into the steaks and let stand half hour. Sauté steaks quickly in the butter, add the Worcestershire, lemon juice and Tabasco. Flame with the Bunratty Meade until the spirit is burned out. Remove the steaks to serving plates, cover with the sauce and garnish with parsley and chives. Delicious with Mushroom Salad With Meade or Warm or Cold Spinach Salad on page 60.
Serves 6.

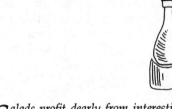

*S*alads profit dearly from interesting dressings, and never more deli-ciously than with ones spiked with Bunratty Meade. These salads can be dressed up-or-down, with the addition of cold sliced or cubed chicken or warm cheese for luncheon, or in smaller portions as starters.

MUSHROOM SALAD WITH MEADE

2 tablespoons/30 ml/1 fl oz lemon
juice
3 tablespoons/45 g/1 ½ fl oz Bunratty
Meade
1 cup/225 g/8 oz fresh mushrooms,
sliced very thin

4 stalks celery, sliced very thin
2 cups/450 g/1 lb shredded Bibb and
Boston lettuce
finely chopped parsley
freshly ground black pepper
lemon slices (for garnish)

Combine lemon juice and Bunratty Meade in jar and shake well. Put mushrooms and celery in shallow dish and pour dressing over. Refrigerate for several hours. Arrange lettuces on 4 salad plates and spoon marinated mushrooms over. Sprinkle with chopped parsley and ground black pepper. Garnish with lemon slices.
Serves 4.

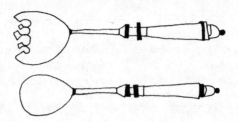

WARM SPINACH SALAD

4 cups/60 g/1 ½ lb fresh spinach
115 g/4oz bacon
¼ cup/60 ml/2 fl oz wine vinegar
1 tablespoon/15 ml/½ fl oz
Worcestershire Sauce

2 tablespoons/30 ml/1 fl oz lemon
juice
¼ cup/60g/2 oz sugar
½ cup/125 ml/4 fl oz Bunratty Meade
freshly ground black pepper

Wash spinach, dry thoroughly, and place in a salad bowl. Sauté the
bacon until crisp, then remove to absorbent paper. Reserve 2
tablespoons of the fat. Add vinegar, Worcestershire, lemon juice
and sugar to the bacon fat and boil for about 3 minutes. Pour over
the spinach. Add Bunratty Meade to the pan and flame. When
flame dies out, pour it over the salad. Crumble the bacon over the
salad, add ground pepper, and toss thoroughly.
Serves 2-4.

SPINACH SALAD WITH MUSTARD MEADE
VINAIGRETTE

⅓ cup/75 ml/2 ½ fl oz oil
1 tablespoons/15 ml/½ fl oz cider
vinegar
3 tablespoons/45 ml/1 ½ fl oz
Bunratty Meade
2 tablespoons/30 ml/1 oz Dijon
mustard

2 tablespoons/30 g/1 oz sesame seeds,
toasted
1 clove garlic or shallot, minced
½ teaspoon freshly ground pepper
4 cups/60 g/1 ½ lb fresh spinach
toasted croutons (optional)

Prepare the Mustard Meade Vinaigrette by placing the first 7
ingredients in a jar and shaking thoroughly to blend. Wash spinach,
dry thoroughly, and place in a salad bowl. Pour over the salad and
toss. Sprinkle with toasted croutons, if desired.
Serves 2-4.

CHICKEN-BERRY SALAD WITH RASPBERRY MEADE VINAIGRETTE

4 tablespoons/60ml/2 fl oz olive oil
2 tablespoons/30 ml/2 fl oz raspberry vinegar
2 tablespoons/30 ml/2 fl oz Bunratty Meade
¼ teaspoon salt
freshly ground pepper, to taste

4 boneless chicken breasts
2 tablespoons/30 g/1 oz butter
4 cups/60 g/1 ½ lb mixed arugula, red-leaf, and bibb lettuce
2 cups/1 pint mixed raspberries and blackberries

Prepare Raspberry Meade Vinaigrette by placing the first 5 ingredients in a jar and shaking to blend thoroughly.

Place chicken between 2 sheets of plastic wrap (cling film) and pound thin. Heat butter or oil in a fry pan and lightly brown the chicken, 3-5 minutes on each side. Remove and cool.

Wash and thoroughly dry the lettuces. Divide onto 4 salad plates. Thinly slice the chicken and divide onto the lettuces. Divide the berries over the chicken and pour the Raspberry Meade Vinaigrette over.

Serves 4.

CRATLOE HILLS SALAD

4 small rounds Cratloe Hills Sheep's Cheese (or similar goat's cheese)
¼ cup/60 ml/2 fl oz olive oil

¾ cup/175 g/6 oz white bread crumbs
4 cups/60 g/1 ½ lb mixed lettuce
Raspberry Meade Vinaigrette Dressing

Place the cheese in a small bowl and pour half of the olive oil over the top. Turn the cheese and pour remaining oil over. Stir cheese rounds gently to coat. Refrigerate for 4-6 hours.

Preheat oven to 400° F/200° C/Gas Mark 6.

Place the bread crumbs in a small bowl. Remove the cheese from the oil and dredge in the crumbs. Transfer the cheese to a lightly greased baking sheet and bake, without turning, until lightly browned, about 10 minutes.

Divide the lettuces onto 4 serving plates and toss lightly with the Raspberry Meade Vinaigrette Dressing. Remove the warm cheese from the oven and place one round on top of the lettuce.

Serves 4.

HEATHER AND HONEY SPARE RIBS

½ cup/125 ml/4 fl oz soy sauce
¼ cup/60 ml/2 fl oz tomato catsup
½ cup/125 ml/4 fl oz Bunratty Meade
2 cloves garlic or shallots, finely chopped

1.8 kg/4 lb spare ribs
2 onions, thinly sliced
½ cup/125 ml/4 fl oz water
1 tablespoon/15 ml/½ fl oz honey

Preheat oven to 350° F/180° C/Gas Mark 4.

Prepare marinade by mixing together the soy sauce, catsup, Bunratty Meade, garlic or shallots. Reserve the marinade. Arrange ribs in a flat roasting pan and cover with onions and water. Cover with foil and bake for 1 hour. Drain and place in the marinade for 4-5 hours. Reserve 2 tablespoons/30 ml/1 fl oz marinade for basting.

Preheat oven to 350° F/180° C/Gas Mark 4.

Mix together the honey and reserved marinade. Arrange marinated ribs in a flat roasting pan, cover with the sauce, and bake further for 30-35 minutes. Raise heat to 450° F/230° C/Gas Mark 8 for the last 5 minutes.
Serves 6-8.

PARKNASILLA PORK CHOP ROAST

6 pork chops, about ¾-inch/2 cm thick, trimmed
¼ cup/60 g/2 oz sifted flour
2 teaspoons salt
⅛ teaspoon pepper
1 tablespoon/15 ml/½ oz Dijon mustard

1 tablespoon/15 g/½ oz brown sugar
6 pineapple slices
6 onion slices
½ cup/125 ml/4 fl oz pineapple juice
¼ cup/60 ml/2 fl oz honey
¼ cup/60 ml/2 fl oz Bunratty Meade

Preheat oven to 350° F/180° C/Gas Mark 4.

Trim pork chops of excess fat. Coat chops in mixture of flour, salt and pepper. Melt some of the trimmed fat in a heavy skillet and

brown the chops. Remove to a shallow, ovenproof baking dish. Spread with the mustard and brown sugar. Top each chop with a pineapple and onion slice. Mix together the pineapple juice, honey and Bunratty Meade and pour over the chops. Bake for 30 minutes covered; remove cover and bake further for 30 minutes. Delicious with Meade Applesauce or Cranberry Meade Applesauce.
Serves 6.

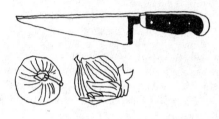

MEADE APPLESAUCE

6 medium-sized cooking apples
¼ cup/60 ml/2 fl oz Bunratty Meade
¼ cup/60 ml/2 fl oz water

2 tablespoons/30 g/1 oz butter
1 tablespoon/15 ml/½ fl oz lemon juice
sugar to taste

Wash, core and quarter apples. Stew apples in Bunratty Meade and water until pulpy. Remove skins. Beat until smooth, add butter, sugar and lemon juice. Serve warm with Parknasilla Pork Chop Roast, goose or duck, or cold as a dessert.
Serves 6-8.

CRANBERRY MEADE APPLESAUCE

4 tart cooking apples
¾ cup/175 g/6 oz whole cranberries
½ cup/125 ml/4 fl oz Bunratty Meade

¼ cup/60 ml/2 fl oz water
½ cup/125 g/4 oz sugar

Wash, core and quarter apples. Combine with cranberries in a saucepan, add Bunratty Meade and water, cover and cook over low heat until apples are mushy (about 25-30 minutes). Stir frequently to prevent sticking. Add sugar and continue to cook until fully reduced. Remove from heat and cool for 30 minutes.

Blend in a food processor 10-15 seconds, then refrigerate for 1-2 hours before use.
Yield: 2 cups.

BRIAN CRONIN'S MEDALLIONS OF PORK

¼ cup/60 g/2 oz butter
½ onion, finely chopped
pinch dried rosemary
⅔ cup/ 150 ml/5fl oz Bunratty Meade
1 cup/ 250 ml/8 fl oz demi-glaze
1 tablespoon/15 ml/ ½ fl oz honey
⅔ cup/ 150 ml/5 fl oz Irish Mist
Liqueur

2 tablespoons/30 ml/1 fl oz heavy cream
1 pork fillet (about 750g/1 ½ lb)
2 tablespoons/60 g/1 oz seasoned flour
4 nettle or spinach leaves (blanched in boiling water)
pinch of paprika

Make sauce first by melting 1 tablespoon/15 g/½ oz butter in a sauté pan. Add onion and rosemary and cook until onion is soft. Add half of the Meade and reduce for one minute. Add demi-glaze and bring to a boil. Add honey and remainder of the Meade. Finally add Irish Mist, cream and correct seasonings.

Cut pork fillets into 12 slices. Flatten and dust lightly with the seasoned flour. Melt remaining butter in a sauté pan and cook fillets for about 5 minutes, or until cooked through. Arrange 3 fillets on plates and pour the sauce over. Garnish with nettle or spinach leaves and top with a little cream and paprika. Before serving, glaze under the grill/broiler to lightly brown the sauce. Serve with Joaney's Garden Potatoes.

Serves 4.   *from the Blue Haven Restaurant, Kinsale, Co Cork*

JOANEY'S GARDEN POTATOES

This rather unorthodox recipe is Brian Cronin's narrative version, but one that is easily adapted by even the most inexperienced cook:

'Joaney was a famous Kinsale lady whose garden on Compass Hill, overlooking the town and harbour, boasted the finest crop of potatoes in the land. The potatoes (about 450g/1lb) are parboiled, cooled and skinned. They are then grated to give slivers of cold potato. Seasonings (salt and freshly ground pepper) and chopped chives (about 2 tablespoons/60 g/1 oz) are added with a little flour (about 2 tablespoons/60 g/1 oz). The potato mixture is added to a hot pan and a potato cake covering the whole face of the pan is formed (approx 1- inch/2.5 cm thick). The cake is turned over in the pan, giving it a lovely brown face! Slice and serve with Brian Cronin's Medallions of Pork, or with your favourite meat.'

DESSERTS

BUNRATTY APPLE TART

4 medium cooking apples, cored and sliced
¼ cup/60 g/2 oz sugar
2 tablespoons/30 ml/1 fl oz Bunratty Meade
1 cup/225 g/8 oz flour

¾ cup /175 g/ 6 oz butter or margarine
1 tablespoon/30 g/½ oz sugar
1 egg yolk
2 tablespoons/30 ml/1 fl oz water

Preheat oven to 350° F/180° C/Gas Mark 4.

Arrange sliced apples in the bottom of a greased 8-inch/20 cm pie plate. Sprinkle with the sugar and Bunratty Meade.

Make a pastry crust by blending the remaining ingredients to form a soft dough. Turn onto a floured board, knead and roll to cover the pie plate. Crimp the edges. Bake for 45-50 minutes, or until the crust is nicely browned. Serve warm with an Irish farmhouse cheddar cheese, or whipped cream.
Serves 8.

IRISH MIST

BANTRY BAY SHRIMP TOAST

1 package cream cheese (225 g/8 oz), softened
1 small can shrimp (115 g/4 oz), rinsed and drained
¼ cup/60 ml/2 fl oz mayonnaise
2 tablespoons/30 ml/1 fl oz Irish Mist Liqueur

1 tablespoon/15 ml/½ oz lemon juice
1 tablespoon/15g/½ oz finely minced parsley
1 package sliced party rye bread (450g/1lb), toasted
225 g/8 oz fresh shrimp, washed and shelled

In a medium bowl, combine first 6 ingredients and mix well. Toast bread, spread with shrimp mix, and brown lightly under the grill/broiler. Place 1 whole fresh shrimp on top of each and serve immediately. (Recipe can be doubled.)
Serves 20-25 as hors d'ouvres.

CELTIC OYSTERS ROCKEFELLER

¼ cup/30 g/2 oz shallots, chopped
¼ cup/30 g/2 oz celery, chopped
3 sprigs parsley
1 cup/225 g/8 oz butter or margarine, softened
1 medium clove garlic, chopped
¼ teaspoon each chervil and tarragon
½ teaspoon each salt and fennel
2 slices bread, broken in pieces
freshly ground pepper to taste
dash Tabasco sauce
¼ cup/60 ml/2 fl oz Irish Mist Liqueur
1 cup /225 g/8 oz fresh spinach, chopped
24 oysters on half shell, cleaned and separated from the shell
rock salt

Preheat oven to 450° F/230° C/Gas Mark 8.

Combine all ingredients, except spinach and oysters, in a blender. Blend, scraping sides, until mix is smooth. Cover each oyster with spinach. Top with one rounded teaspoon of blended ingredients. Place on a bed of rock salt in a large shallow baking pan or ovenproof platter. Bake for 10 minutes. Place 4 oysters on serving plates and serve immediately.

Serves 6 as a starter.

SWORD OF ODIN

1 cup/250 ml/8 fl oz Irish Mist Liqueur
2 tablespoons/30 ml/1 fl oz cooking oil
2 cloves garlic, crushed
½ cup/125 ml/4 fl oz lemon juice
½ teaspoon oregano
2 teaspoons salt
10-12 grinds fresh black pepper
750g/1 ½ lb lamb, cut into 1½-inch/3.5 cm cubes
18 cherry tomatoes
2 green peppers, cut into 1 ½-inch/3.5 cm pieces
18 small white onions, peeled and boiled for 5 minutes

Combine first seven ingredients in a small saucepan and simmer for about 5 minutes. Pour over lamb and marinate overnight.

Divide lamb, tomatoes, peppers and onions onto 6 skewers and grill until lamb is cooked to desired degree. Serve with brown rice or grilled potatoes.

Serves 6.

CONNEMARA CHICKEN

4 boneless chicken breasts
¼ cup /60 g/2 oz onions, finely chopped
¼ cup/60 g/2 oz mushrooms, finely chopped
¼ cup/60 g/2 oz bacon
1 tablespoon/15 g/½ oz butter or margarine

¼ cup/60 ml/2 fl oz Irish Mist Liqueur
¼ cup/60 g/2 oz flour
1 cup/250 ml/8 fl oz chicken stock
½ cup/125 ml/4 fl oz heavy (double) cream
salt and pepper
fresh parsley (for garnish)

Sauté or poach chicken as desired. Sauté onions, mushrooms, and bacon in butter. Add Irish Mist and flour and cook for 2 minutes. Add stock, stir until smooth, and simmer for 15 minutes. Add cream, salt and pepper to taste, and continue to cook for 3-5 minutes. Place cooked chicken breast on plate and cover with Irish Mist sauce. Garnish with fresh parsley. Delicious with white or brown rice and a fresh green salad.

Serves 4.   *from Gallagher's Boxty House, Dublin*

TULACH MHÓR LAMB STEW

1 teaspoon thyme
1 ½ teaspoons salt
½ teaspoon freshly ground pepper
2 cups/500 ml/ 1 pint chicken stock
¾ cup/175 ml/6 fl oz Irish Mist Liqueur

3 tablespoons/45 ml/1 ½ fl oz lemon juice
4 large potatoes, peeled and sliced
900 g/2 lb stewing lamb, cut into 1-inch/2.5 cm cubes
3 onions, sliced
finely chopped parsley

Preheat oven to 350° F/180° C/Gas Mark 4.

Combine thyme, salt and pepper in a small bowl and set aside. Mix chicken stock, Irish Mist and lemon juice together and set aside. In a buttered 3-quart/3 litre casserole, place a third of the potatoes. Cover with a third of the lamb and a third of the sliced onions. Sprinkle with half of the seasonings. Repeat layers, seasoning in-between, ending with the onions. Add the liquid, cover, and bake for 1 ½ -2 hours or until lamb is tender. Sprinkle with parsley.

Serves 6-8.

CENTURION LAMB

2.2 kg/5 lb/1 leg of lamb
2 large garlic cloves, slivered
1 teaspoon salt
½ teaspoon freshly ground pepper

1 lemon, thinly sliced
1 cup/250 ml/8 fl oz mint jelly with leaves
¾ cup/175 ml/6 fl oz Irish Mist Liqueur

Preheat oven to 350° F/180° C/Gas Mark 4.

Make slits in meat and insert garlic slivers. Sprinkle all over with salt and pepper. Place in a shallow baking pan and arrange lemon slices all over the surface of the lamb. Roast for 1 hour 15 minutes.

Mix mint jelly and ½ cup/125 ml/4 fl oz Irish Mist together to a sauce consistency. Remove lamb from oven, discard lemon slices, and baste with the sauce. Return to oven and continue baking for 45 minutes or until meat thermometer reaches 175° F/90° C. Baste every 15 minutes. Remove from oven.

Heat remaining Irish Mist, pour over roast and carefully ignite. Remove roast to serving platter and allow to relax. Heat pan drippings, stirring thoroughly, and serve as a sauce for the lamb.
Serves 6-8.

ROMAN ROAST OF PORK

2 kg/4 lb/1 pork loin roast
1 large clove garlic, cut into slivers
2 cups/500 ml/1 pint orange juice
1 cup/250 ml/8 fl oz Irish Mist Liqueur

½ teaspoon ground cloves
1 teaspoon ground ginger
1 tablespoon/15 ml/½ fl oz cooking oil
1 teaspoon salt
½ teaspoon pepper

Cut slits into pork and insert garlic. In a large bowl combine orange juice, Irish Mist, cloves and ginger. Place pork in the marinade and refrigerate several hours or overnight.

Preheat oven to 350° F/180° C/Gas Mark 4.

Remove pork from marinade and reserve. In a dutch oven or heavy pot, brown roast well in the cooking oil. Sprinkle with salt and pepper and turn several times for even browning. Transfer pork to roasting pan, pour marinade over all, and bake for 2-3 hours or until meat is tender. For best results, use meat thermometer. Strain sauce and serve with the meat. Delicious with Cinnamon Apples.
Serves 6.

CINNAMON APPLES

4 baking apples, cored
½ cup/115 g/4 oz brown sugar
1 teaspoon cinnamon
¼ teaspoon nutmeg
¼ cup/60 g/2 oz slivered almonds

¼ cup/60 g/2 oz seedless raisins
¼ cup/60 ml/2 fl oz Irish Mist Liqueur
¾ cup/175 ml/6 fl oz water
juice of 1 lemon
¼ teaspoon finely grated orange rind

Preheat oven to 350° F/180° C/Gas Mark 4.

Peel 1-inch/2.5 cm from top of each apple after removing the core. Place apples in 2-quart/2 litre baking dish. Mix brown sugar, cinnamon, nutmeg, almonds and raisins together and fill center of each apple with mixture. Mix Irish Mist, water, lemon juice and orange rind together and pour over the apples. Bake for 35-40 minutes or until apples are tender. Serve apples in individual dishes with sauce spooned over each one. Delicious with pork.
Serves 4.

SALMON JANETTE

1 tablespoon/15 g/½ oz butter
2 salmon fillets (about 175 g/6 oz each)
salt and freshly ground white pepper
1 teaspoon fresh ginger, grated
¼ cup/60 ml/2 fl oz Irish Mist Liqueur
½ cup/115 g/4 oz sugar
½ cup/125 ml/4 fl oz water

½ cup/125 ml/4 fl oz white wine vinegar
½ cup/125 ml/4 fl oz red wine vinegar
2 lemons
2 limes
2 oranges
2 sprigs fresh fennel (for garnish)

Preheat oven to 350° F/180° C/Gas Mark 4.

Butter an ovenproof baking dish and place in the salmon fillets. Season with salt and pepper. Sprinkle the grated ginger over the fillets and pour in the Irish Mist. Cover and bake for about 15 minutes.

Meanwhile, dissolve the sugar in a small saucepan with the water and white wine vinegar. Allow to caramelize and become deep brown in colour. Remove from heat and carefully add in the red wine vinegar, stirring to dissolve completely. Remove two wedges from each of the fruits (for garnish), then the juices. Add juices to the sauce, return to heat and reduce to a glazing consistency.

Check salmon is firm to touch. Remove to warm serving plates, pour sauce over, and place under the grill/broiler for a few minutes to glaze. Garnish with lemon, lime and orange wedges and sprigs of fresh fennel.

Serves 2.   *from the White House, Kinsale, Co Cork*

LOBSTER WITH IRISH MIST

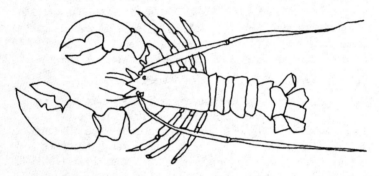

2 lobsters (450-500 g/1-1 ¼ lbs)	½ cup/125 ml/4 fl oz Irish Mist
2 lemons	Liqueur
½ cup/115 g/4 oz butter	2 cups/500 ml/1 pint heavy (double)
¼ cup/60 g/2 oz shallots, chopped	cream
freshly ground black pepper	chopped fresh parsley (for garnish)

Wash lobsters in cold water for a few minutes. With a sharp pointed knife pierce lobster through the head, approximately 1-inch/2.5 cm back from the eyes. Plunge into boiling water, reduce heat and cook for about 15 minutes.

Meanwhile, grate 1 lemon. Put butter, shallots, pepper, juice and rind of lemon into small pan. Bring to a boil, add Irish Mist and flame. Continue to cook for 2 minutes until reduced. Add cream, stir and remove from heat. When lobsters are cooked, remove from pot and allow to cool slightly. Remove meat from claws and tail (reserve tail shell). Return sauce to heat, bring to second boil, add lobster meat and cook for 1-2 minutes. To serve, spoon lobster meat and sauce into shell, garnish with chopped parsley and half a lemon.

Serves 2.   *from the Ante Room Restaurant, Dublin*

BRIAN CRONIN'S MISTIC MONK

750 g/1 ½ lb monkfish
2 tablespoons/30 ml/1 fl oz lemon juice
black pepper
2 tablespoons/30 g/1 oz seasoned flour
½ cup/125 g/4 oz butter

½ cup/115 g/4 oz peeled tomatoes, chopped
¼ cup/60 g/2 oz onions, chopped
12 large lettuce leaves
2 tablespoons/30 ml/1 fl oz Irish Mist Liqueur
½ cup/125ml/4fl oz cream

Bone the monkfish and slice into medallions (about ½-inch/1 cm each). Season with touch of lemon juice and black pepper and toss in seasoned flour. Melt butter in a sauté pan and cook fish until golden brown (about 3-4 minutes). Remove and keep warm in a low oven. Reserve the pan juices. Quickly add to the sauté pan the tomatoes, onions, lettuce and Irish Mist and cook for 2-3 minutes. Add cream and cook until almost boiling.

Remove fish from oven and arrange in a circular fashion around the edges of 2 serving plates. Pour sauce over the fish medallions and leave a well in the centre for remaining sauce. Serve with boiled potatoes and a fresh green salad.

Serves 2.   *from the Blue Haven Restaurant, Kinsale, Co Cork*

DESSERTS

Some simple toppings made with Irish Mist can turn vanilla ice cream, frozen yogurt or plain pound cake into an elegant, dazzling dessert. Or, try Irish Mist combined with fresh fruit or chocolate to create a luscious mousse or a sinfully rich cheesecake. Serve in Irish crystal for an even more impressive effect.

IRISH MIST AND STRAWBERRIES

2 cups/450 g/1 lb fresh strawberries, sliced

1 cup/250 ml/8 fl oz Irish Mist Liqueur

Put strawberries in a small bowl and pour over Irish Mist. Allow to marinate for about 1 hour. Serve alone in 4 brandy snifters, or as a topping.

Serves 4.

IRISH MIST CHEESECAKE

¾ cup/175 g/6 oz digestive biscuits, crumbled
¼ cup/60 g/2 oz butter
8 envelopes gelatine
½ cup/125 ml/4 fl oz warm water
500 g/1 ¼ lb cream cheese

½ cup/125 ml/4 fl oz Irish Mist Liqueur
5 large eggs, separated
¾ cup/175 g/6 oz sugar
1 cup/250 ml/8 fl oz heavy (double) cream, lightly whipped

Mix biscuit crumbs with melted butter and press into 9-inch/22.5 cm springform tin. Soak gelatine in cold water and strain when softened. Add to warm water to dissolve. Add Irish Mist. Cream the cheese in large bowl, add egg yolks and sugar. Beat until mixture is smooth. When thoroughly creamed, mix in gelatine. Fold in whipped cream. Whip egg whites and fold into mixture. Turn into crust and chill for at least 2 hours.

Serves 12.   *from the Dún Aonghasa Restaurant, Kilronan, Aran Islands*

MOCHA MIST MOUSSE

8 squares/225 g/8 oz semi-sweet chocolate
2 tablespoons/30 g/1 oz sugar
1 tablespoon/15 g/½ oz instant coffee powder
¼ cup/60 ml/2 fl oz Irish Mist Liqueur

⅓ cup/75 g/2 ½ oz butter, cut into pieces
4 eggs, separated
whipped cream (for garnish)
fresh strawberries or mint (for garnish)

Put chocolate, sugar and instant coffee in the top of a double boiler over hot water. Stir until melted and smooth. Remove from heat and stir in the Irish Mist. Stir butter in a piece at a time. Beat egg yolks, then carefully stir into mixture. Cool slightly. In a separate bowl, beat egg whites until stiff peaks form. Fold into cooled chocolate mixture until well combined. Pour into 6 sherbet dishes. Refrigerate for at least 6 hours before serving. Garnish with whipped cream, fresh raspberries or fresh mint.

Serves 6.

IRISH MIST TRUFFLES

18 squares/500 g/18 oz bittersweet (dark) chocolate, melted
¾ cup/175 ml/6 fl oz heavy (double) cream

½ cup/125 ml/4 fl oz Irish Mist Liqueur

Place chocolate in a double boiler and melt over low heat. Add half of the cream slowly and whisk into the chocolate. As it starts to thicken, pour in the rest of the cream and whisk gently until smooth. Whisk in the Irish Mist. Remove from heat and chill in the refrigerator until firm (about an hour or more).

When thoroughly chilled, roll into bite-sized balls, using a spoon or small ice cream scoop. Work quickly so the mixture doesn't warm up too much. (If so, refrigerate again for a few minutes.) Truffles can be rolled in cocoa powder, finely ground nuts, or dipped in melted chocolate to cover completely. Store in refrigerator in a single layer for up to a week.

Yield: 3 dozen.   *from Roscoff's Restaurant, Co Antrim*

*M*atthew D'Arcy, Chef/Proprietor of Darcy's Restaurant, Kenmare, County Kerry, holds the prestigious title of Master Chef from the World Master Chef Association. But when it comes to desserts, he enjoys the delicate taste of a native liquer like Irish Mist, here in this soufflé which can be made up to a day in advance.

CHILLED IRISH MIST SOUFFLE

5 envelopes gelatine
2 tablespoons/30 ml/1 fl oz Irish Mist
Liqueur
6 egg yolks
1 cup/225 g/8 oz confectioners' sugar
1 pint/500 ml/20 fl oz heavy (double)
cream, whipped

6 egg whites
¼ cup/60 g/2 oz confectioners' sugar
¼ cup/60 g/2 oz almonds, toasted
and chopped
¼ cup/60 ml/2 fl oz heavy (double)
cream, whipped
fresh cherries (for garnish)

Tie a 2-inch band of waxed paper around the outside of two 1x3-inch/7.5 cm soufflé dishes. Soak the gelatine leaves in cold water to cover. Warm the Irish Mist in a small pan. Place the egg yolks and sugar in a large bowl and place over a pan of hot water or bain-marie. Whisk vigorously until the mixture thickens and whitens. Remove from heat, add the dissolved gelatine and whisk from time to time until the mixture is nearly cold. Fold in Irish Mist. Lightly whip the cream. Whisk egg whites until nearly stiff. Add remaining confectioners' sugar and continue mixing until the mixture is stiff. Fold the whipped cream into the egg mixture and then fold in the whites.

Pour the mixture into prepared soufflé dishes and chill at least 1 hour. Remove the paper from the moulds and coat the exposed sides with the almonds. Garnish with the whipped cream and fresh cherries. Can be made a day in advance.

Serves 6.

Chapter IV
Celtic Cider

Like so many other natural beverages, cider is one of our most traditional drinks. The process of pressing apples, extracting and fermenting the juice has produced a refreshing alcoholic drink since ancient times. Cider was popular with the ancient Greeks and Romans, and later in Christian times monastic orders were considered to have made an important contribution to the development of orchards for the purpose of cider making. Of all fruits, the apple plays the most important part in legend and folklore, with its hues of green, gold and russet inspiring tales and traditions that have been passed down through generations of Irish.

During the Middle Ages, cider was a popular beverage in Ireland, particularly in rural areas. Water supplies in large towns were often unreliable, and tea and coffee were as yet unknown in Europe. As a result, alcoholic beverages, including cider, were consumed by worker and master alike as the process of brewing produced a safe, bacteria-free drink.

The Anglo-Norman period saw the introduction of orchards in Munster, with this tradition of cultivation later reinforced by English settlers under the 'Plantation of Munster'. Apple trees were imported from England along with a group of men skilled in the job of planting new orchards and cultivating the crops to yield a fruitful harvest.

Undoubtedly, Irish cider benefitted from the Anglo-Norman influence, and by the 17th century, a time known as the 'First

Golden Age of Cider', there were over 350 named varieties of cider apple growing throughout Ireland. Because most farmers could not afford the large outlay of land and slow return from an orchard, most apple orchards were found on large farms and estates. The area around Limerick soon became famous for cider, as did Cork, Kerry, Waterford and South Tipperary.

Clonmel, though, came to be the home of cider production in Ireland. Situated in a rich and fertile tract of land, Clonmel continues to produce the greater bulk of the best quality of cider apples for the industry. In 1935, a cider-making company began commercial production in Dowd's Lane, when a local man, William Magner, set up his own business. In 1937, he amalgamated with H. P. Bulmer and Company, from whose name the famous Bulmer's label is derived. Ownership of the label is now with Showerings Ireland Ltd, Clonmel, who maintain the natural and traditional fermentation process so important even in modern production.

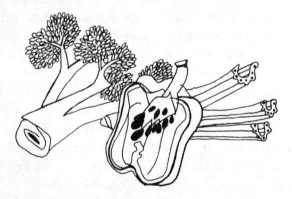

Today Showerings produces a wide range of ciders to satisfy a variety of tastes: the most popular is Bulmers Original, a traditional medium sweet vintage cider with a rich golden colour; Strongbow is a medium dry cider, stronger in alcohol than Bulmers, and lighter in colour; and Linden Village, which contains the same alcohol level as Strongbow but is less dry in flavour and darker in colour. For celebratory purposes, three sparkling ciders are produced: Vervier, Michelle and Palais D'Or.

In Ireland, cider has emerged as a truly sophisticated drink which many consumers regard as a natural alternative to wine. The two, in fact, undergo the same fermentation process, can be

served in similar situations, and drunk with equal enjoyment. For years cider has been a popular ingredient in many forms of cuisine, a particular favourite among the Celts, Bretons and Normans. Today, cooking experts consider it to be as desirable and flavoursome as wine in a wide range of recipes. It is the basis of a number of excellent sauces and is especially delicious with pork. Steeping a ham in cider, particularly at Christmas time, is a much loved and honoured tradition, but cooks need not wait for a holiday to experiment with the number of different styles of cider — sweet, medium and dry; sparkling and still.

CHICKEN NORMANDE

1.8 kg/4 lb/1 whole roasting chicken
3 slices white, crustless bread, cubed
2 tablespoons/30 g/1 oz butter or margarine
450 g/1 lb cooking apples, peeled, cored and chopped
1 tablespoon/30 g/½ oz sugar
pinch ground cinnamon

salt and freshly ground black pepper
8 slices streaky bacon, chopped
1 cup/250 ml/8 fl oz Bulmers Cider
2 tablespoons/30 ml/1 fl oz cooking oil
½ cup/125 ml/4 fl oz chicken stock
½ cup/125 ml/4 fl oz dairy sour cream

Preheat oven to 400° F/200° C/Gas Mark 6.

Wash the chicken, inside and out, and pat dry. Heat the butter and lightly brown the cubed bread. Remove to a small bowl. Sprinkle the apples with sugar and sauté with the cinnamon, salt and pepper in the same pan. When the apples have begun to soften, remove them and mix with bread cubes. Add the chopped bacon and moisten with 2 tablespoons/30 ml/1 fl oz of the cider. Stuff the mixture into the prepared chicken and secure with poultry pins or truss. Rub the bird with the oil, sprinkle with salt and pepper, and cover loosely with aluminium foil. Put into a roasting pan and bake 25-30 minutes.

Reduce heat to 375° F/190° C/Gas Mark 5.

Mix half of the remaining cider together with the chicken stock, warm slightly, and baste chicken several times during cooking. Roast an additional 45-50 minutes. When done, remove bird to a hot serving plate.

Pour off pan juices to a small saucepan, scraping the meat from the pan, and add the remaining cider. Mix well and boil rapidly on top of stove to reduce and thicken. Lower heat, stir in the sour cream, and re-heat until hot. Do not boil. Serve in separate sauce boat with the whole chicken.

Serves 4.

*N*ext to chicken, pork must be numbered among the most versatile of white meats. It is especially delicious when accompanied by apples, tart fruit relishes, chutneys and stuffings. Cider is probably the most natural and flavoursome way to enhance the sweet taste of pork, and hearty potatoes are always a perfect addition. Each of the following recipes uses pork, apples and cider with the most subtle variations. A number are all-in-one dishes. Experiment with your own special touches!

PORK CHOPS BRAISED IN CIDER WITH POTATOES

4 boneless centre-cut pork chops
2 tablespoons/30 ml/1 fl oz cooking oil
2 small onions, peeled and sliced
2 cooking apples, cored, peeled and sliced
½ teaspoon marjoram

½ teaspoon sage
salt and freshly ground pepper
1 tablespoon/15 g/½ oz butter or margarine
1 cup/250 ml/8 fl oz Bulmers Cider
450 g/1 lb potatoes, peeled and sliced
2 tablespoons/30 g/1 oz butter

Preheat oven to 375° F/190° C/Gas Mark 5.

Trim the chops of any excess fat. Heat the oil in a sauté pan and gently brown the chops on both sides. Transfer to an ovenproof casserole dish. In the same oil, lightly cook the sliced onions until soft and golden brown. Add the apples and soften, but do not let brown. Add the marjoram, sage, salt and pepper to taste. Add the cider, mix well and bring to the boil before pouring over the chops.

Spread the potatoes evenly over the meat. Dot with butter. Cover the casserole and bake for 30 minutes. Remove cover and bake a further 30 minutes to brown the potatoes.

Serves 4.

HONEY GLAZED LOIN OF PORK

900 g/2 lb pork loin roast, boned and rolled

2 tablespoons/30 ml/1 fl oz honey

1 ½ teaspoons dried sage leaves

½ teaspoon freshly ground black pepper

3 slices lean bacon

½ cup/125 ml/4 fl oz Bulmers Cider

½ cup/125 ml/4 fl oz beef broth

8 baking potatoes

Place the pork in a casserole dish. Mix together the honey, sage, and pepper in a small pan and heat to thin the honey. With a basting brush, coat the meat all over with the honey mixture. Cover and refrigerate for 12 hours, turning occasionally.

Preheat oven to 350° F/180° C/Gas Mark 4.

Remove pork from refrigerator about 30 minutes before roasting. Lay the strips of bacon over the meat, pour on the cider, and bake for 60-75 minutes, or test with a meat thermometer. Place potatoes in the oven at the same time.

When the meat is done, remove to a warmed platter. Remove any fat from the pan juices and put the pan on the top of the stove over medium heat. Add beef broth and stir continuously to remove any bits of meat. Reduce to sauce consistency (about ½ cup/125 ml/4 fl oz), and sieve. When ready to serve, spoon the sauce over the meat. Serve with baked potatoes, a fresh green vegetable and Apple Chutney .

Serves 8.

APPLE CHUTNEY

2 green apples, peeled, cored, and finely chopped

½ lemon, seeded and finely chopped

⅓ cup/75 g/2 ½ oz finely chopped onion

½ cup/115 g/4 oz chopped red pepper

½ cup/115 g/4 oz golden raisins

2 tablespoons/30 g/1 oz freshly grated ginger

1 clove garlic, pressed

⅓ cup/75 ml/2 ½ fl oz cider vinegar

⅔ cup/150 g/5 oz brown sugar

⅛ teaspoon cayenne pepper

½ teaspoon salt

Combine all the ingredients in a large, heavy, non-reactive saucepan. Stir well, bring to a boil, then reduce heat and simmer gently, uncovered. Stir frequently until ingredients have thickened (about 45-60 minutes). Taste and correct seasonings. Allow to cool before serving. Chutney can be stored, covered and refrigerated, for up to 2 weeks.

Yield: 1 pint/500 ml/20 fl oz.

CIDER GLAZED BAKED HAM

1.8 kg/4 lb pre-cooked or canned ham	1 teaspoon dry mustard
12-15 whole cloves	¼ cup/60 ml/2 fl oz orange or
¼ cup/60 g/2 oz brown sugar	pineapple juice
	¾ cup/175 ml/6 fl oz Bulmers Cider

Preheat oven to 350° F/180° C/Gas Mark 4.

Score the ham and stud with cloves. Mix brown sugar and mustard together , then add the juice and ½ cup/125 ml/4 fl oz of cider. Stir thoroughly to make a paste. Spread over the ham and bake about 1 hour, basting occasionally. When ham is cooked, remove to a warm platter. Add additional cider to the pan, scrape, and boil the drippings. Add more juice or water, if necessary, and cook to a sauce consistency. Serve in a sauceboat with the carved ham.

Serves 8-10.

PHEASANT IN CIDER

2 pheasants	2 tablespoons/30 g/1 oz flour
1 bay leaf	2 tablespoons/30 g/1 oz butter
1 sprig parsley	½ cup /125 ml/4 fl oz Bulmers Cider
salt and black pepper	2 tablespoons/30 ml/1 fl oz Calvados
1 onion, sliced	(Apple Brandy)
2 sticks celery, chopped	¼ cup/60 ml/2 fl oz heavy (double)
2 cooking apples, peeled, cored and chopped	cream

Joint the breast by first removing the legs, then cut away the two breast sections down and along the backbone. (Leave the flesh on the bone so that it won't shrink during cooking.) Cut off the wing sections.

Put the pheasant carcasses, necks and giblets into a large pot with bay leaf, parsley, salt and pepper. Cover with cold water, cover the pan, and simmer over low heat for 20 minutes to make a stock.

Preheat oven to 325° F/170° C/Gas Mark 3.

In a small bowl, mix together the onion, celery (reserve the leaves) and apples. Melt the butter in a heavy fry pan. Coat the pheasant joints lightly with a little flour and fry in the butter over medium heat until golden brown. Remove meat from pan. Add the onion/celery/apple mixture and cook for a further 5 minutes. Remove pan from heat, stir in remaining flour, then gradually blend in the cider, Calvados and 1 cup/250 ml/8 fl oz of the pheasant stock. Return pan to heat and simmer for 5-8 minutes.

Place the meat in an ovenproof casserole dish. Pour the sauce over to cover (add more stock, if necessary), season with salt and pepper, cover and bake for 45 minutes.

At the end of the cooking time, remove the pheasant to a warmed platter. Put casserole on top of stove and bring sauce to boil. Stir in the cream and adjust seasonings. Serve the breasts on warmed plates with sauce poured over. Garnish with sliced unpeeled apple wedges and celery leaves.

Serves 4.

LAMB STUFFED WITH APPLES AND BAKED IN CIDER

1.8 kgs/4 lb/1 leg of lam, boned
½ lemon, juiced
4 cooking apples, peeled, cored and sliced
2 tablespoons/30 g/1 oz sugar
3 whole cloves

2 cloves garlic, sliced
2 teaspoons ground ginger
salt and freshly ground black pepper
2 tablespoons/30 ml/1 fl oz olive oil
1 pint/500 ml/20 fl oz Bulmers Cider

Preheat oven to 400° F/200° C/Gas Mark 6.

Rub the meat, inside and out, with the lemon juice. Grate the lemon peel and sprinkle on the meat. Lay the apples on the inside of the lamb, sprinkle with sugar, dot with the cloves and roll up. Tie with string or secure with long skewers. Insert the garlic slices under the skin, then rub the whole of the outside with a mixture of the ginger, salt and pepper. Lastly, brush the outside of the meat with the olive oil. Place in an oven roaster and cook for about 30 minutes. Lower the heat to 375°F/190°C/Gas Mark 5 and continue to roast for a further 2 hours.

Meanwhile, heat the cider and baste the lamb with it about every 15 minutes. When the meat is cooked, put it on a hot serving dish. Transfer the roasting pan to the top of the stove, pour off any excess fat, add remaining cider and mix well. Reduce by half, scraping the bits of meat from the pan. Season to taste, sieve, and serve the gravy separately in a sauce boat.

Serves 6.

DUCK WITH CIDER

2.2 kg/5 lb duck
salt and pepper
2 apples, cored and sliced
1 ½ cups/350 ml/12 fl oz Bulmers Cider

2 tablespoons/30 g/1 oz butter
2 tablespoons/30 g/1 oz flour
¾ cup/175 ml/6 fl oz cream

Preheat oven to 325° F/170° C/Gas Mark 3.

Rub duck inside and out with salt and pepper. Fill the cavity with apple slices and secure with skewers. Place on a rack in a roasting pan and pour cider over. Roast for 2 ½ hours, basting every 20 minutes. When finished cooking, remove to a warmed serving platter.

Strain the cooking liquid into a saucepan. Make a roux with the butter and flour and gradually add to the strained liquid. Bring to a boil. Cook the sauce for 2-3 minutes, stirring continuously, or until it is smooth and thick. Correct seasonings, then stir in the cream gently and warm through. Serve the sauce in a separate sauceboat along with the duck.

Serves 4.

WILD RABBIT CIDER STEW

1 rabbit, skinned
¼ cup/60 ml/2 fl oz lemon juice
2 slices bacon
2 tablespoons/30 g/1 oz seasoned
flour
1 onion, diced
1 carrot, diced

1 teaspoon dried thyme
1 bay leaf
½ cup/115 g/4 oz chopped parsley
2 tomatoes, peeled and chopped
salt and pepper
1 tablespoon/15 g/½ oz sugar
1 cup/250 ml/8 fl oz Bulmers Cider
1 cup/250 ml/8 fl oz water

Cut the rabbit into serving pieces and soak in cold water and lemon juice for 2-3 hours.

Preheat oven to 350° F/180° C/Gas Mark 4.

Drain the rabbit and dry thoroughly. Fry the bacon gently until fat runs. Remove bacon and keep warm. Toss the rabbit pieces in seasoned flour and fry until golden brown. Add onion, carrot, thyme, bay leaf, parsley and tomatoes. Cook gently for 15-20 minutes. Add salt, pepper, sugar, cider and water and bring to a boil. Continue to boil for 3-5 minutes. Remove to an ovenproof casserole dish and bake for 60-75 minutes, or until rabbit is tender. Serve with Irish Apple Potato Cakes.

Serves 4.   *from the Blue Haven Restaurant, Kinsale, Co Cork*

IRISH APPLE POTATO CAKES

450 g/1 lb potatoes, quartered
2 apples, cored, peeled and sliced
½ cup/115 g/4 oz chopped parsley

4 tablespoons/60 g/2 oz butter
salt and freshly ground pepper

Boil potatoes and stew apples in separate pans until both are soft. Cool for 5-10 minutes. Mash the potatoes, add the stewed apple, half the butter and seasonings. Pat together to form little patties. (Add a little flour, if necessary, to hold together.) Sauté in the remaining butter until browned and crisp. Serve with Wild Rabbit Cider Stew and a fresh green salad.

from the Blue Haven Restaurant, Kinsale, Co Cork

SOMERSET PIE

4 boneless chicken breasts, cubed	1 cup/250 ml/8 fl oz Bulmers Cider
4 slices streaky bacon, diced	½ cup/115 g/4 oz button mushrooms,
1 carrot, chopped	sliced
1 onion, sliced	salt and pepper to taste
2 sticks celery, sliced	1 tablespoon/15 g/½ oz cornstarch
½ red pepper, chopped	2 pastry crusts
1 cup/250 ml/8 fl oz chicken stock	1 egg yolk, beaten

Place chicken and bacon in saucepan along with the carrot, onion, celery, pepper, cider and stock. Bring to a boil, cover, reduce heat and simmer for 1 hour. Add mushrooms and season to taste. Blend the cornstarch with a little cold water and add to the pan to thicken. Return to boil, stirring continuously. Remove from heat and cool.

Preheat oven to 400° F/200° C/Gas Mark 6.

Prepare half recipe for pastry crusts according to recipe on page 43. Line a 9-inch/22.5 cm pie plate with bottom crust, spoon in the mixture, cover with top crust. Trim and crimp the edges. Make some slits in the top crust to allow steam to escape. Brush with beaten egg yolk. Bake for about 45 minutes, or until top is golden brown. If crust browns too soon, cover with waxed paper until cooking time is reached.

Serves 6.

*D*ublin Coddle, an ancient and truly 'inner city dish,' was Jonathan Swift's favourite meal. It is actually a local breakfast stew with no parameters as to its ingredients. According to Feargal O hUiginn, Chef-Proprietor of Oisin's Restaurant in Dublin, 'Coddle is traditionally consumed after a Saturday night "on the jar" (also known as having consumed too much Guinness!). It is a dish which allows artistic licence for each cook, and if you ask any Dublin cab driver how he or his wife makes it, you'll find each driver has his own recipe. One taxi driver I spoke to recently puts tomatoes in his Coddle, and allows them to break down. He calls this Red Coddle.' Ohuighinn also recommends good quality pork sausages, well-cured gammon of ham, strong cider, and 'strong, tear-jerking onions.' He recommends you 'serve it with brown soda bread, more Guinness or red wine, depending on the time of day. Close your eyes and you're in Dublin anytime between 1600 and 1995!'

DUBLIN CODDLE

900 g/2 lb pork sausages
900 g/2 lb gammon of ham
(unsmoked)
3 onions, diced
4 large cooking apples, peeled, cored
and chopped

900 g/ 2lb potatoes, peeded and cubed
¾ cup/175 ml/6 fl oz Bulmers Cider
¼ cup/60 g/2 oz chopped parsley
1 quail's egg per person (optional)
fresh parsley and cherry tomatoes,
halved (for garnish)

Cut the sausages into quarters and cube the gammon into similar size. Place sausages, ham, onions, and apples in large pot and cover with water. Bring to the boil. Add potatoes, cider and parsley and simmer, covered, until potatoes are tender, about 35-40 minutes.

Preheat oven to 350° F/180° C/Gas Mark 4.

Portion out the Coddle into 6 or 8 individual ovenproof bowls. Crack a quail's egg into the middle of each bowl, allowing room for it to set down into the stock. Bake until egg whitens, about 10 minutes. Remove bowls from oven, garnish with freshly chopped parsley and cherry tomatoes.
Serves 6-8.

SEATROUT WITH APPLE AND CIDER SAUCE

4 fillets of seatrout, skinned and boned
1 golden apple, peeled, cored and
halved
freshly ground white pepper
2 shallots, finely chopped
1 tablespoon/15 g/½ oz butter

½ bottle Bulmers cider
½ cup/125 ml/4 fl oz fish stock
½ cup/125 ml/4 fl oz heavy (double)
cream
1 cucumber, diced
1 carrot, diced

Preheat oven to 350° F/180° C/Gas Mark 4.

Lay out fish fillets, flesh side down, and place an apple slice on top. Season with pepper. Fold ends of fish over the apple, envelope-style, and place folded side down onto a greased baking pan. Bake in preheated oven for 6-8 minutes.

While the fish is baking, prepare the sauce. Dice the remaining half of the apple. In a sauté pan, sweat off the shallots in the butter with the diced apple. Add the cider and fish stock and reduce by half. Add cream and reduce to a sauce consistency. To serve, arrange seatrout on a serving plates, garnish with cucumber and carrot, and pour sauce around.
Serves 4.   *from the Hibernian Hotel, Dublin*

BRETON FISH STEW

1 tablespoon/15 ml/½ fl oz cooking oil
1 onion, sliced
2 cloves garlic, crushed
2 carrots, sliced
1 stick celery, sliced
 2 tablespoons/30 g/1 oz flour
1 cup/250 ml/8 fl oz fish stock
1 cup/250 ml/8 fl oz Bulmers Cider
grated rind of 1 lemon

1 bouquet garni
450 g/1 lb cod fillets, cubed
salt and freshly ground black pepper
1 ½ cups/350 g/ ¾ lb pearl onions
2 tablespoons/30 g/1 oz butter
1 tablespoon/15 g/½ oz sugar
1 cup/225 g/ ½ lb button mushrooms
1 tablespoon/15 g/½ oz chopped parsley

Heat the oil in a large frying pan. Add onions, garlic, 1 carrot and celery and sauté for 5 minutes. Add the flour and blend, stirring continuously. Gradually stir in the stock, cider, lemon rind and bouquet garni. Bring to the boil and simmer for 10 minutes. Strain into a clean pan, add the cod, season and cook for 10-12 minutes or until the fish begins to flake.

Meanwhile, pour boiling water over the pearl onions and leave for 5 minutes. Drain, add fresh cold water, and boil gently for about 15 minutes.

Heat butter and sugar in a large frying pan. Add pearl onions, mushroooms and remaining carrot and cook for 10 minutes. Stir in the fish mixture, sprinkle with parsley and serve immediately. Accompany with garlic bread and a fresh green salad.
Serves 4.

DESSERTS

WEST COUNTRY CIDER CAKE

1 ¼ cups/300 g/10 oz white flour
1 teaspoon ginger
¾ cup/175 g/6 oz butter

¾ cup/175 g/6 oz sugar
1 tablespoon/15 ml/½ fl oz honey
2 eggs
¼ cup/60 ml/2 fl oz Bulmers Cider

Preheat oven to 325° F/170° C/Gas Mark 3.

Sift the flour with the ginger. Cream the butter, sugar and honey in a small bowl. Beat the eggs and add them with the flour to the creamed mixture. Stir for 3-5 minutes to blend well. Add the cider and blend again.

Grease and line an 8-inch/20 cm round cake pan. Pour batter in and bake for about 1 hour and 20 minutes, or until browned on top. Test with wooden pick. Cool on wire rack and remove paper. Serve with Sweet Cider Sauce or Honey Cider Cream.
Serves 8.

SWEET CIDER SAUCE

½ cup/125 ml/4 fl oz heavy (double) cream
¼ cup/60 ml/2 fl oz Bulmers Cider
2 teaspoons Irish Mist Liqueur

1 egg, separated
2 tablespoons/30 g/1 oz confectioners' sugar

Whisk the cream until it is frothy and slightly stiff, then gradually add the cider, whisking continuously. Add the Irish Mist and blend well. Separate the egg. Beat the yolk and the sugar together until slightly frothy, then combine with the cream and cider mixture. Beat the egg white until stiff and fold it in gently. Pour into a serving dish, cover with plastic wrap and chill until needed. If it remains in the refrigerator for too long, it may need to be lightly whisked again before use.

HONEY CIDER CREAM

½ cup/115 g/4 oz confectioners' sugar
½ cup/115 g/4 oz butter

1 tablespoon/15 ml/½ fl oz honey
¼ cup/60 ml/2 fl oz Bulmers Cider

Cream together the sugar and butter. Add the honey and cider and beat until smooth. Spread over the top of the Cider Cake.

CIDER AND WALNUT GATEAU

½ cup/115 g/4 oz sultanas
1 cup/250 ml/8 fl oz Bulmers Cider
1 cup/225 g/8 oz white flour
pinch of salt
1 teaspoon mixed spice**

½ cup/115 g/4 oz butter
½ cup/115 g/4 oz sugar
2 eggs
1 tablespoon/15 ml/½ fl oz honey
¼ cup/60 g/2 oz walnuts, chopped

Soak the sultanas in the cider overnight.

Preheat oven to 350° F/180° C/Gas Mark 4.

Sift together the flour, salt and spices into a small mixing bowl. Add the remaining ingredients and beat until well-blended. Pour into a greased and floured 2 lb loaf tin, smooth over the top, and bake about 1 hour. Reduce temperature to 325°F/170°C/Gas Mark 3 and cook a further 20 minutes, or until it tests done with a wooden pick. Cool on a wire rack. Slice and serve with butter.

Serves 8-10.

**See recipe on page 26.

PEARS IN CIDER

6 large hard pears	1 vanilla pod
2 cups/500 ml/1 pint Bulmers Cider	1 tablespoon/15 g/½ oz cornstarch
½ cup/115 g/4 oz sugar	toasted flaked almonds
2 sticks cinnamon	whipped cream

Preheat oven to 250° F/130° C/Gas Mark ½.

Peel pears, but do not remove stalks. Place them into a shallow ovenproof casserole. Put cider, sugar, and cinnamon into a small saucepan and bring to a boil. Add vanilla pod and pour mixture over the pears. Cover casserole with lid or foil and bake for 3 hours. Turn pears half way through baking.

Remove pears to serving dish and cool slightly. Pour the cooking liquid into a small saucepan, discarding the vanilla pod and cinnamon sticks. Blend the cornstarch with a little water to form a smooth paste. Add to the liquid and bring to a boil, stirring continuously until the mixture is thick and syrupy. Pour this over the pears. Allow to cool, then baste the pears again with the syrup. Chill thoroughly. When ready to serve, sprinkle with toasted flaked almonds and a dollop of whipped cream.

Serves 6.

CIDER BAKED APPLES WITH TOASTED MUESLI

4 cooking apples	¼ cup/60g/2oz muesli
1 cup/250 ml/8 fl oz Bulmers Cider	heavy (double) cream or whipped
1 tablespoon/15 g/½ oz butter	cream

Preheat oven to 375°F/190°C/Gas Mark 5.

Wipe and core the apples. Cut through the skin around the centre of each apple. Pour the cider into a shallow baking pan. Lightly grease each apple with butter and stand upright in the cider. Bake for 40 minutes, basting 2-3 times during cooking.

After 15 minutes, put muesli in a shallow ovenproof pan and bake, uncovered, until it has toasted lightly. At the end of the cooking time, divide the toasted muesli onto 4 service plates, place an apple on top and pour the juices over. Serve with cold heavy cream or whipped cream.

Serves 4.

Chapter V
Sweet Irish Creams

While the taste of Irish-made mead, whiskey, beer and cider has been pleasing palates for centuries, the cream liqueurs of Ireland have been on the market for less than two decades. You might say, though, that their inception was as inevitable as tomorrow's rain, for it was only a matter of time before two of Ireland's greatest treasures—the cream from its rich dairy pastures and the spirits from its finest distilleries—would be brought together to create a third. It's the marriage of these two traditions that accounts for the unparalleled success of Irish cream liqueurs in the world's market.

R&A Bailey launched its Original Irish Cream in 1974, after discovering the secret that would allow milk to be separated into double cream and blended with natural flavours, Irish whiskey and neutral spirits. Steeped in Irish history and lore, it was named after the Dublin pub 'The Bailey', a favorite haunt of James Joyce, and its bottle design is based on an old Irish whiskey brand, Red Breast.

The origins of Baileys, in fact, assume near mythic proportions, with some claiming that the liqueur is based on a tradition in the West of Ireland where fresh cream was added to Irish Whiskey, then gently stirred and sipped. The idea of a bottled cream liqueur with smoothness, depth and a rich luxurious character is what makes Baileys so popular. For those whose taste run to less consumption of calories and fat, there's new Baileys Light, with 33% fewer calories and 50% less fat.

Soon to follow Baileys into the marketplace, Carolans Irish Cream, named for the celebrated 17th century blind harpist Turlough O'Carolan, was developed in 1978. It, too, combines aged Irish spirits and rich double cream, but adds a touch of

honey to give it a distinctively subtle flavour that differentiates it from others. Honey is an appropriate ingredient in a drink produced in Clonmel, County Tipperary, as the name Clonmel is derived from the Gaelic Cluain Meala, meaning the 'Vale of Honey.' Carolans calls itself the 'Finest Irish Cream.'

St Brendan's Irish Cream Liqueur, with production based at Rossdowney, Northern Ireland, is named for the 6th century Irish monk who set sail to discover the Garden of Eden. It claims to be 'truly Irish, and probably the only Irish cream liqueur which is made from genuine Irish whiskey — no preservatives, no artificial flavours or colourings.' St Brendan's calls itself 'Superior Irish Cream Liqueur.'

The pleasure that Irish creams provide in drinks, straight-up, on the rocks, or mixed with other liqueurs, has led to a whole range of exciting dessert recipes as well. As inevitable as their inception, it was only a matter of time before adventurous chefs on the look out for fresh inspiration would add a splash of Baileys to a soufflé or mousse, a few tablespoons of Emmets or St Brendan's to a cheesecake or parfait, or a cup of Carolans to cookies or custard. Innovative bakers, pastry chefs and dessert makers have discovered that Irish cream liqueurs are now the magical, indispensable ingredient the world has been waiting for for years.

IRISH CREAM MOUSSE

4 eggs	1 egg white
½ cup/115 g/4 oz sugar	1 cup crème anglaise
½ teaspoon vanilla extract (essence)	½ cup/125 ml/4 fl oz Baileys Irish Cream
½ cup/115 g/4 oz flour	2 envelopes gelatine
1 cup/250 ml/8 fl oz heavy (double) cream	½ cup/125 ml/4 fl oz water

Preheat oven to 425° F/220° C/Gas Mark 7.

To prepare the sponge, whisk eggs and sugar together until it peaks. Add vanilla, then fold in flour. Turn into a 10-inch/25 cm springform tin and bake in preheated oven for about 10 minutes.

Prepare crème anglaise according to directions on page 28. Semi-whip the cream and whisk the egg white. Dissolve the gelatine in the water and add to crème anglaise. Add the Baileys and allow to cool. Mix cream, egg white and egg custard together gently.

To assemble the mousse, remove the sides from the springform tin. Slice through the sponge horizontally, and return bottom half to the tin. Replace ring. Pour half the mixture over the cake, place other half of the sponge over it, then pour remaining Baileys/custard over top. Refrigerate for 3-4 hours, or until set. To serve, remove the sides and cut into wedges.

Serves 8-10. *from Mc Grattan's Restaurant, Dublin*

*A*rt buff Arthur French O'Carroll, proprietor of Dublin's Lane Gallery Restaurant, enjoys serving avant garde dishes with colourful garnishes and exciting flavours — a perfect complement to the restaurant's changing exhibit of paintings. Another testament to culinary innovation, and one of the most sought after desserts at his pretty mews restaurant, is a chilled mousse made with Baileys Irish Cream and blueberries.

BAILEYS MOUSSE WITH BLUEBERRIES

1 lemon	½ cup/125 ml/4 fl oz Baileys Irish Cream
1 egg	
5 egg whites	¼ cup/60 g/2 oz unsalted butter, melted
1 cup/225 g/8 oz sugar	⅛ teaspoon cream of tartar
	2 cups/450 g/1 lb fresh blueberries

Grate the rind of the lemon and put it in the top of a double boiler. Squeeze the juice from the lemon and add it to the rind. Whisk the egg, 1 egg white, ¾ of the sugar and Baileys together and put it in the top of the double boiler. Set it over simmering water. Cook the mixture, stirring continuously until it thickens, 12-15 minutes. Do not overcook or it will curdle. Remove the double boiler from the heat and mix in the butter. Set the top of the double boiler in a larger bowl filled with ice and let the mixture cool. Whisk occasionally.

To prepare the meringue, put the remaining egg whites and the cream of tartar in a bowl and beat them until soft peaks form. Add a little of the remaining sugar and continue beating the egg white, gradually adding the rest of the sugar until stiff peaks have formed and the meringue is glossy.

Stir a few heaping spooonfuls of the meringue into the cooled Baileys mixture to lighten it. Fold in the remaining meringue and add all but ½ cup/115 g/4 oz of the rinsed blueberries. Spoon the mousse into parfait glasses and chill for at least 1 hour before serving. Garnish each serving with a few of the reserved blueberries.

Serves 6.

BAILEYS CHOCOLATE MOUSSE

12 squares/350 g/12 oz milk chocolate
1 cup/250 ml/8 fl oz milk
2 tablespoons sugar
⅓ cup/75 ml/ 2 ½ fl oz Baileys Irish Cream

3 cups/75 ml/2 ½ fl oz heavy (double) cream
5 envelopes gelatine
2 egg whites

Boil together the chocolate, milk, sugar, Baileys and 1 cup/250 ml/8 fl oz cream. Set aside and allow to cool. Semi-whip the remaining cream. Melt the gelatine in enough water to thoroughly dissolve. Whip the egg whites.

When chocolate is cooled, add it to the semi-whipped cream. Add in the gelatine and gently fold in the egg whites. Pour into 8 individual ramekins, refrigerate and allow to set.

Serves 8.   *from the Cottage Loft, Restaurant, Kinsale, Co Cork*

EMMETS COFFEE ALMOND SOUFFLE

3 eggs, separated
⅓ cup/75 g/2 ½ oz sugar
½ cup/125 ml/4 fl oz strong black coffee
½ cup/125 ml/4 fl oz Emmets Irish Cream

½ oz gelatine
¼ cup/60 ml/2 fl oz hot water
1 ¼ cup/300 ml/½ pint heavy (double) cream
whole toasted almonds
almond flavoured liqueur (optional)

Place egg yolks, sugar and coffee in a bowl and whisk until thick and frothy. Fold in Emmets. Dissolve gelatine in hot water and add to mixture. Pour into a soufflé dish and refrigerate until slightly set.

Whisk egg whites until stiff. Gently fold into the mixture. Whisk cream until slightly thickened and fold in. Serve with whole toasted almonds and a spash of almond flavoured liqueur, if desired.
Serves 6.

EMMETS GAELIC CUSTARD

2 egg yolks
2 tablespoons/30 g/1 oz sugar
¼ cup/60 ml/2 fl oz Emmets Irish Cream

whipped cream
cherries (for garnish)

Beat egg yolks and sugar in a double boiler until thick and creamy. Beat in Emmets. Spoon into sherbert glasses, top with a tablespoon of whipped cream and a cherry. Serve immediately.
Serves 2.

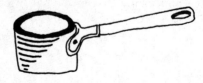

*L*ike so many other Irish chefs, Patrick Brady of the Westbury Hotel's Russell Room Restaurant has found the sweet creams of Ireland are perfectly combined with another staple, Brown Soda Bread, to create a sumptuous ice cream. Here is his version which is simplicity itself.

PATRICK BRADY'S BROWN BREAD ICE CREAM

¾ cup/175 g/6 oz brown soda bread crumbs

½ cup/115 g/4 oz brown sugar

¼ cup/60 g/2 oz crushed almonds

½ gallon/½ litre vanilla ice cream

1 cup/250 ml/8 fl oz Baileys Irish Cream

Preheat oven to 425° F/220° C/Gas Mark 7

Combine bread crumbs, sugar and almonds. Place on a baking sheet and cook for 10-15 minutes, or until golden brown. Remove and cool. Crush the mixture into small pieces. Beat the ice cream to thick consistency. Add Baileys and bread crumb mixture to the ice cream. Mix well. Freeze in individual parfait glasses or plastic freezer container.

*B*runo Schmidt, Head Chef at the prestigious Park Hotel, Kenmare, County Kerry, likes the combination of Baileys and chocolate in this elegant raisin ice cream log.

BAILEYS RAISIN CHOCOLATE LOG

⅔ cup/150 ml/5 fl oz water

1 cup/225 g/8 oz sugar

8 eggs separated

2 cups/500 ml/1 pint heavy (double) cream, whipped

½ cup/115 g/4 oz raisins

¼ cup/60 ml/2 fl oz Baileys Irish Cream

⅓ cup/75 g/2½ oz dark chocolate

2 egg yolks

½ cup/125 ml/4 fl oz heavy (double) cream

¼ cup/60 g/2 oz butter

¼ cup/60 g/2 oz confectioners' (icing) sugar

⅓ cup/90 g/3 oz cocoa

Place water and sugar together in a heavy pan and boil for about 4 minutes. Remove from heat, mix in the egg yolks and Baileys and whisk until cold. Whip the cream and fold in. Beat the egg whites until almost stiff and fold in. Add the raisins and stir gently. Pour into an ice cream log mould or bombe and freeze until firm.

To make the granache, melt the chocolate in a double boiler, add remaining ingredients and blend thoroughly. Cool.

Remove the ice cream from the mould, coat with the chocolate granache, then return to refrigerator or freezer until ready to serve. *Serves 8.*

BAILEYS BLANC-MANGE

2 oz Carrageen moss	1 cup/250 ml/8 fl oz Baileys
2 cups/500 ml/1 pint milk	honey (to taste)

Before using, pick over and wash the Carrageen in lukewarm water to remove any small stones that are often attached. (In Irish, Carrageen means 'small stone,' suggesting that the moss should be washed thoroughly to remove any.) Place the Carrageen and the milk in a heavy pot and simmer over low heat until the mixture thickens, about 15-20 minutes. Stir occasionally, making sure it does not boil up and overflow. When sauce is thickened, remove from heat and place in a blender to liquidize. Blend to smooth. Add Baileys and honey, blend a further 30 seconds, and place in a mould or individual sherbet dishes to set and chill.

Serves 4-6. *from Oisín's Restaurant, Dublin*

PROFITEROLES

½ cup/15 g/4 oz butter	pinch salt
1 ¼ cups/300 ml/½ pint water	4 eggs, beaten
¾ cup/175 g/6 oz flour	

Preheat oven to 400° F/200° C/Gas Mark 6.

Put the butter and water in a saucepan and melt over low heat. When butter has melted bring to a full boil. Add flour and salt immediately and beat until mixture forms a thick paste. Remove from heat and leave until just warm. Gradually add eggs, beating thoroughly after each addition. The paste should be smooth and glossy.

Place spoonfuls of mixture on a greased baking tray, leaving room between each spoonful to allow for rising. Bake for 30 minutes, or until well risen and crisp. Remove and make a slit in each one to

allow steam to escape. Cool on a wire rack. Fill with whipped cream and top with Baileys Hot Chocolate or Coffee Sauce.
Yield: 20-25 small buns.

HOT CHOCOLATE SAUCE

3 tablespoons/45 g/1 ½ oz cornstarch
2 cups/500 ml/1 pint water
2 tablespoons/30 g/1 oz sugar
1 square/30 g/1 oz semiwseet chocolate

2 cups/500 ml/1 pint heavy (double) cream
2 tablespoons/30 ml/1 fl oz Baileys Irish Cream

In a small saucepan blend the cornstarch to a smooth paste with a little of the water. Add the remaining water. Stir over medium heat until boiling. Reduce the heat and simmer gently for 2 minutes, then add the sugar. Mix well. Break the chocolate into pieces and add to the sauce. Continue stirring over low heat until the chocolate has melted. Add the cream and Baileys. Heat gently, without boiling, for a further 2 minutes. Serve hot.

HOT COFFEE SAUCE

1 cup/225 g/8 oz brown sugar
¼ cup/60 ml/2 fl oz water
2 ½ cups/625 ml/1 ¼ pints black coffee

¼ cup/60 ml/2 fl oz Baileys Irish Cream

In a small saucepan stir the sugar in the water over medium heat until dissolved. Increase the temperature and boil the syrup until it is a pale golden colour. Add the coffee and continue boiling until the sauce thickens slightly and turns syrupy. Remove from heat and stir in the Baileys. Serve hot.

BAILEYS CREAM CHEESECAKE

1 ½ cups/350 g/ 12 oz digestive biscuits
1 cup/225 g/8 oz butter
5 envelopes gelatine
225 g/8 oz cream cheese
¾ cup/175 g/6 oz sugar

2 cups/500 ml/1 pint heavy (double) cream
¼ cup/60 ml/2 fl oz Baileys Irish Cream
whipped cream
fresh strawberries (for garnish)

Place biscuits in plastic bag and crush finely. Melt the butter and mix together with the crushed biscuits. Press into the base of an 8-inch/20cm flan pan. Dissolve the gelatine in cold water.

Beat together the cheese and sugar. Whip the cream, add Baileys, and fold into the creamed cheese mixture. Add gelatine. Pour the cheese mixture on top of the biscuit base. Allow to set for 1-2 hours. Garnish with rosettes of cream and fresh fanned strawberries.

Serves 8.   *from the Bon Appetit Restaurant, Malahide, Co Dublin*

*T*his *Northern Ireland version of Irish Cream Cheesecake is one of the specialties at Joey and Margaret Erwin's 'Macduff's Restaurant,' located in the cellars of Blackheath House, their country house hotel in Aghadowey, near Coleraine, County Derry. Using a local Irish cream, St Brendan's, the cheesecake is always featured on the sweet menu of Macduff's, the 1994 recipient of the Egon Ronay 'Dessert of the Year' Award. Try this award-winner for yourself.*

ST BRENDAN'S CREAM CHEESECAKE

1 ¼ cups/300 g/10 oz crushed digestive biscuits
2 tablespoons/30 ml/1 oz chocolate milk powder
½ cup/115 g/4 oz butter, melted
1 envelope gelatine
2 tablespoons/30 ml/1 fl oz cold water
2 egg whites

½ cup/115 g/4 oz sugar
1 ¼ cups/300 ml/½ pint heavy (double) cream
1 cup/225 g/8 oz cream cheese
⅓ cup/75 ml/2 ½ fl oz St. Brendan's Irish Cream
fresh strawberries or chocolate curls, for garnish
whipped cream, for garnish

Mix together the biscuits, chocolate milk powder and melted butter and press into a 9-inch/22.5 cm springform tin. Chill while preparing the filling.

Dissolve the gelatine in cold water. Whip the egg whites with the sugar until peaks form. Whip the cream. In a small bowl, cream the cheese, add the gelatine and Irish Cream, and fold in the whipped cream. Pour cheesecake mixture into chilled base and refrigerate for at least 2 hours. To serve, cut into slices and garnish with fresh fruit, chocolate curls or whipped cream.

Serves 8.

COFFEE AND WALNUT GATEAU

⅓ cup/ 75 g/2 ½ oz butter or
margarine
¾ cup/175 g/6 oz sugar
2 eggs
½ teaspoon coffee extract (essence)
1 cup/225 g/8 oz flour

2 teaspoons baking powder
½ teaspoon salt
¼ cup/60 ml/2 fl oz milk
¼ cup/60 ml/2 fl oz Baileys Irish
Cream
½ cup/115 g/4 oz walnuts, chopped

Preheat oven to 350° F/180° C/Gas Mark 4.

Cream the margarine and sugar until light and fluffy. Add the eggs, one at a time, beating well after each addition. Stir in the coffee extract.

Sift together the flour, baking powder and salt. Add to the egg mixture, alternating with the milk and Baileys, until well-blended. Fold in the walnuts. Grease and line with waxed paper two 8-inch/20 cm cake tins. Pour the batter into the tins and bake for 35-40 minutes, or until well risen and springy to the touch. Turn onto wire racks and cool. Remove waxed paper and cool completely. Fill and frost with Baileys Coffee Icing.
Serves 10-12.

BAILEYS COFFEE ICING

½ cup/115 g/4 oz unsalted butter
1 cup/225 g/8 oz confectioners' sugar,
sifted
¼ cup/60 ml/2 fl oz Baileys Irish
Cream

1 teaspoon coffee extract (essence)
3 tablespoons/45 ml/1 ½ fl oz milk
8-10 walnut halves (for decoration)

Cream the butter and confectioners' sugar. Mix well, stir in the Baileys and coffee extract. Add just enough milk to make the icing smooth and of a spreading consistency. Fill and frost the layers and sides. Decorate with walnut halves.

APPLE FLAN WITH BAILEYS

1 cup/225 g/8 oz flour
pinch salt
¾ cup/175 g/6 oz butter
2 egg yolks
⅓ cup/75 g/2 ½ oz sugar
2 teaspoons cinnamon

3-4 firm eating apples, peeled and
cored
generous amount of Baileys Irish
Cream
2 tablespoons/30 g/1 oz brown sugar
whipped cream (optional)

Preheat oven to 400° F/200° C/Gas Mark 6.

Combine flour, salt, butter, egg yolks, cinnamon and sugar to make pastry crust. Roll out and line an 8-inch/20cm spring form tin. Slice apples and arrange, overlapping, on the pastry. Pour in the Baileys generously (to cover all the apples). Sprinkle with brown sugar. Bake for 25-30 minutes. Serve warm with whipped cream, if desired.

Serves 6-8. *from the Enniscoe House, Ballina, Co Mayo*

BAKED APPLES WITH CAROLANS

1 tablespoon/15 g/½ oz walnuts, chopped	½ teaspoon cinnamon
1 tablespoon /15 g/½ oz sultanas, chopped	4 cooking apples, washed and cored
2 tablespoons/30 g/1 oz sugar	½ cup/60 g/2 oz butter, cut up
	¼ cup/60 ml/2 fl oz Carolans Irish Cream

Preheat oven to 350° F/180° C/Gas Mark 4.

Mix together the nuts, sugar, sultanas and cinnamon and fill the centre of each apple with the mixture. Place small pats of butter on each apple, cover with aluminum foil, and bake in an oven-proof dish for about 25 minutes. To serve, put an apple on each serving plate and pour Carolans Irish Cream over each one. Serve immediately.

Serves 4.

STRAWBERRY AND BAILEYS FOOL

900 g/2½ lb strawberries, hulled (reserve 6 for garnish)	½ cup/125 ml/4 fl oz Baileys Irish Cream
2 cups/500 ml/1 pint heavy (double) cream	confectioners' sugar (for dusting)

Chill 6 champagne glasses in refrigerator while preparing the dessert.

Place the strawberries in a blender, purée for a few seconds, then sieve. Whip the cream until stiff peaks form, add half the strawberry purée and the Baileys. With a piping bag or spoon, divide the strawberry/cream mix into the bottom quarter of the champagne glasses. Pour the fruit purée in to half way up, then alternate layers of strawberry/cream and fruit purée to fill. Garnish with sliced reserved strawberries and sprinkle with confectioners' sugar. Serve immediately.

Serves 6.   *from the Hibernian Hotel, Dublin*

BREAD PUDDING WITH CAROLANS CREAM SAUCE

350 g/12 oz Irish soda bread with fruit,
or bakery raisin bread, cut into
1-inch/2.5 cm pieces
3 cups/750 ml/1 ½ pints milk
¾ cup/175 ml/6 fl oz Carolans Irish
Cream Liqueur
1 ½ cups/350 g/12 oz sugar

4 eggs
1 tablespoon/15 ml/½ fl oz vanilla
½ cup/115 g/4 oz raisins
1 cup/225 g/8 oz confectioners' sugar
½ cup/115 g/4 oz butter
1 egg, beaten
¼ cup/60 ml/2 fl oz Carolans Irish
Cream

Preheat oven to 350° F/180° C/Gas Mark 4.

To make the pudding, combine bread, milk and Carolans in a large bowl. Cover and refrigerate for at least 1 hour, stirring occasionally. In a mixing bowl, whisk together sugar, eggs and vanilla. Pour into bread mixture, stirring to blend. Fold in raisins. Butter a 9x13-inch/22.5x32.5 cm baking tin. Spoon pudding into baking dish. Bake until set, about 50-60 minutes, or until golden brown. Cool.

To make the sauce, combine confectioners' sugar and butter in the top of a double boiler. Stir constantly over simmering water until sugar dissolves and mixture is hot. Remove from heat. Whisk in egg and continue to beat until mixture has cooled to room temperature. Stir in Carolans.

Preheat grill/broiler. Line a jelly roll (Swiss roll) pan with aluminium foil. Cut pudding into 8-10 squares. Place pieces on foil. Spoon sauce over all. Broil until pudding is bubbly on top. Serve warm or at room temperature.

Serves 8-10.

CAROLANS RICH RICE PUDDING

½ cup/115 g/4 oz uncooked white rice
1 cup/250 ml/8 fl oz milk
1 cup/250 ml/8 fl oz heavy (double) cream
¼ cup/ 60 g/2 oz sugar
2 strips lemon rind

¾ teaspoon ground cinnamon
⅓ cup/75 ml/2 ½ fl oz Carolans Irish Cream
½ cup /125 ml/4 fl oz heavy (double) cream, whipped
1 cup /225 g/8 oz fresh strawberries or peaches, sliced

Soak rice in cold water for 30 minutes, then drain. Heat milk and cream together in top of a double boiler. Add rice, sugar, lemon rind and cinnamon. Cook over simmering water, about 1 hour, stirring occasionally until liquid is absorbed. Remove lemon pieces, stir in Carolans, and cook an additional 15 minutes. Remove from heat and cool for about 30 minutes. Refrigerate until well chilled, about 3 hours. Spoon into dessert dishes and garnish with whipped cream and fresh fruit.
Serves 4.

CAROLANS IRISH BLONDIES

1 cup/225 g/8 oz sugar
¼ cup/60 g/2 oz butter, softened
1 egg

¾ cup/175 g/6 oz flour
¼ cup/60 ml/2 fl oz Carolans Irish Cream
⅓ cup/75 g/2 ½ oz walnuts, chopped

Preheat oven to 350° F/180° C/Gas Mark 4.

Beat sugar, butter and egg together until light and fluffy. Stir in flour alternately with Carolans. Fold in nuts. Spread mixtue into an 8-inch/20 cm square greased baking tin. Bake 30 minutes until golden and firm on top. Cool fully on wire rack. Cut into 16 squares. (Cookies' flavour improves kept overnight in a cool place.)
Yield: 16 squares.

CAROLANS CHIP COOKIES

½ cup/115 g/4 oz butter
¾ cup/175 g/6 oz light brown sugar
1 egg
1 cup/225 g/8 oz flour
½ teaspoon baking soda

¼ teaspoon salt
⅓ cup/75 ml/2 ½ fl oz Carolans Irish Cream
¾ teaspoon vanilla
¾ cup/175 g/6 oz semi-sweet chocolate morsels

Preheat oven to 375° F/190° C/Gas Mark 5.

Beat butter and sugar together until light and fluffy. Beat in egg. Sift flour with baking soda and salt. Add to butter mixture alternately with Carolans and vanilla. Stir in chocolate pieces. Drop batter by slightly rounded teaspoons on to a greased cookie sheet. Bake 10-12 minutes or until golden. Remove from pan and cool completely on wire racks.

Yield: 3 dozen.

GLOSSARY AND BASIC RECIPES

Bain-marie: literally a water bath, used for gentle cooking, especially of pâtés, terrines, and mousses. The bain-marie is filled with water so that a saucepan placed inside it is surrounded by water. This is kept at the simmering point, in a low-temperature oven, to prevent a crust from forming.

Beurre-clarifié: clarified butter, obtained by heating the butter until it liquifies to remove the milk solids and obtain a clear liquid.

Beurre-manié: equal quantities of butter and flour, kneaded together to form a paste for thickening sauces. The liquid should be below boiling point when the beurre manié is added, a little at a time, beating thoroughly after each addition. The liquid is then brought to boil to thicken.

Bouquet garni: a combination of herbs, usually fresh parsley, thyme, bay leaf and chervil, tied together in a cheesecloth bag during cooking to flavour it. It is removed before serving.

Carrageen moss: a natural Irish seaweed that is celebrated as a folk remedy; also used to thicken puddings, aspics and jellies.

Court bouillon: a seasoned or flavoured stock for cooking fish or vegetables.

Crème anglaise: custard sauce (see page 28 for recipe).

Demi-glaze: a meat glaze extract, achieved by boiling down a meat stock to a syrupy consistency; also called glace de viande.

Julienne: thin, match-like strips of food, especially vegetables.

Mirepoix: finely diced carrots, onions and celery, slowly cooked in butter and seasonings; used as a flavouring for sauces and fillings.

Pâté: a mixture of ground meats, poultry or fish, seasonings; often baked in wine or in a crust.

Poach: to cook food, especially fish, in a liquid just below the boiling point.

Reduce: to reduce the volume of a liquid by boiling, uncovered; used to thicken sauces, stocks or syrups, and to concentrate flavour.

Roux: a mixture of butter and flour cooked together and used as a thickener in sauces.

Trussing: tying the legs and wings of poultry to keep the shape.

Velouté: literally a rich and velvety sauce; made from poultry, veal or fish stock, and white roux.

Vinaigrette: a dressing of vinegar, oil and other seasonings.

BASIC RECIPES

A great number of recipes call for stock for flavouring. A stock, also called bouillon, is used as a base for sauces, mousses and stews and is best if home-made. Stock can be refrigerated for 3-4 days, or frozen indefinitely in small quantities. It is simple to make, and any time the trimmings or bones of fish or meat are left over, a stock can be made to have available for future recipes. Once the stock is made, it can be turned into a demi-glaze by further reducing over high heat until about 1 cup remains. This will be very strong (almost like a prepared bouillon cube) and can be added in small quantities to sauces that need a flavour boost. Demi-glaze can be frozen in an ice cube tray, then stored in freezer bags for individual use.

A court bouillon is used to cook all kinds of fish and shellfish. Fish can be cooked ahead of time and left in the court bouillon to prevent drying out.

Fish stock is also convenient to have on hand as a base for fish sauces, like velouté, for fish mousse and for poaching. Home-made mayonnaise, and both whisked and blender hollandaise are, likewise, easy to make and add a real gourmet touch to recipes requiring them. Basic recipes for all of these essential stocks and sauces are given here.

CHICKEN STOCK

900g-1.4kg/2-3 lb chicken bones, wings, carcasses	1 carrot, chopped
	2 onions, chopped
water to cover the bones (about 3 quarts)	bouquet garni
	1 cup/250 ml/8 fl oz dry white wine
4 stalks celery, chopped	salt and pepper

Combine the chicken and water in a large pot and bring slowly to the boil. Skim the fat occasionally as it comes to the top. Once boiling, reduce the heat to simmer, add the remaining ingredients and cook slowly, about 2 hours. Skim as necessary. Strain the stock through muslin, cool and chill. Remove any fat that comes to the top. Use immediately or freeze in small containers.
Yield: 2-3 quarts.

BROWN STOCK

900g-1.4kg/2-3 lb chicken, beef, lamb or game bones and trimmings	water to cover bones (2-3 quarts)
	¾ cup/175 ml/4 fl ozs red wine
2 tablespoons/30 ml/1 fl oz oil	bouquet garni
2 each onions, carrots, celery stalks, chopped	8 black peppercorns
	½ clove garlic, unpeeled
2 tablespoons/30 ml/1 fl oz tomato paste	

Preheat oven to 450° F/230° C/Gas Mark 8.

Heat the oil in a large roasting pan, add the bones and turn to coat. Place in the oven until the bones start to brown. Add the chopped vegetables, stirring well. Once the vegetables and bones are nicely browned, add the tomato paste and return to oven for a further 5 minutes.

Transfer the bones and vegetables to a large saucepan. Deglaze the pan with 1 cup of water and the wine, scraping up all the juices and pieces of meat. Pour this over the bones and vegetables, cover with more water and bring to the boil. Add the bouquet garni and other spices. Skim occasionally. Simmer for 1 hour, skimming further. Strain the stock through muslin, cool and chill. Skim any fat that comes to the surface. Use immediatley or freeze in individual containers.

Yield: 2 quarts.

FISH STOCK

2 tablespoons/30 ml/1 fl oz butter
1 each onion and carrot, chopped
1 ¼ cups/300 ml/10 fl oz (½ pint)
white wine or vermouth
900g-1.4kg/2-3 lb fish trimmings
(heads, bones, skin)

6-8 sprigs parsley
8-10 peppercorns
1 bay leaf
5 cups water

Heat the butter in a heavy saucepan, add the vegetables and sweat for a few minutes. Add the wine, reduce slightly, then add the fish trimmings and remaining ingredients. Bring to the boil and skim frequently. Reduce heat to simmer, continue to skim, and cook for 25-30 minutes. Cool slightly, then strain stock through muslin. Correct seasonings. Use immediately or freeze in individual containers.

Yield: about 6 cups.

FISH VELOUTE

3 tablespoons/45 g/1½ fl oz each
butter and flour
1 ¼ cups fish stock

½ cup/125 ml/4 fl oz cream
2 egg yolks
salt and pepper

Combine butter and flour and cook over low heat for 2-3 minutes, stirring gently. Gradually pour in the heated fish stock and continue to stir. Blend the cream with the egg yolks, add to the mixture and stir until sauce thickens. Season to taste with salt and pepper.

Yield: 1 ½ cups.

COURT BOUILLON

1 tablespoon/15 g/½ oz butter	4 cups/1 litre/1¾ pints water
2 each carrots, onions, celery stalks, chopped	2 sprigs parsley
	2 bay leaves
1 cup/250 ml/8 fl oz dry white wine	8-10 peppercorns

Melt the butter in a saucepan, add the vegetables, cover and sweat for 8-10 minutes. Add the wine and water and bring to the boil. Add the remaining ingredients and simmer for 15 minutes. Strain and cool. The bouillon is now ready for use in any fish recipe.
Yield: 5 cups.

HOLLANDAISE SAUCE

3 egg yolks	¼ teaspoon salt
1 tablespoon/15 ml/½ fl oz cold water	1 teaspoon lemon juice
½ cup/115 g/4 oz soft butter	pinch white pepper

Combine egg yolks and water in the top of a double boiler and beat with a wire whisk over hot water until fluffy. Add a few spoonfuls of butter and beat until butter has melted and sauce starts to thicken. Continue adding the butter, small portions at a time, stirring constantly. Add the salt, lemon juice and pepper. Sauce can be used immediately or kept warm over lukewarm water.
Yield: 1 cup.

BLENDER HOLLANDAISE

3 egg yolks	pinch white pepper
2 tablespoons/30 ml/1 fl oz lemon juice	½ cup/115 g/4 oz butter, melted
¼ teaspoon salt	

Place egg yolks, lemon juice, salt and pepper in a blender jar. Cover and blend at high speed for 30 seconds. Uncover and begin pouring in the melted butter, a little at a time, until a thick cream is formed. Sauce can be used immediately or kept warm over lukewarm water.
Yield: ¾ cup.

HOME-MADE MAYONNAISE

3 egg yolks, at room temperature
½ tablespoon plus 1 teaspoon wine vinegar
½ teaspoon salt

¼ teaspoon dry mustard
1 ½- 2 cups (1 pint)/7.5 ml good quality olive oil
salt and white pepper

Warm a mixing bowl and dry thoroughly. Beat the egg yolks for 1-2 minutes until thickened. Add vinegar, salt, pepper and mustard and beat again a further minute. Slowly dribble in the oil and continue to beat until at least ½ cup of the oil has been blended. Continue to add the oil until the mixture is thick and looks like prepared mayonnaise. Use immediatley or refrigerate.

Yield: 2 cups.

BLENDER MAYONNAISE

1 egg
2 teaspoons wine vinegar
½ teaspoon salt

1 teaspoon dry mustard
1 cup good quality olive oil

Place egg, vinegar, salt and mustard in a blender jar. Blend on high for 30 seconds. Uncover, dribble in the oil and and blend until mixture emulsifies and thickens (about 1 minute). Use immediately or refrigerate.

Yield : 1 ½ cups.

VINAIGRETTE DRESSING

6 tablespoons/90 ml/3 fl oz olive oil
2 tablespoons/30 ml/1 fl oz wine vinegar
salt and freshly ground black pepper

1 tablespoon/15 ml/½ fl oz Dijon mustard
garlic or shallot clove, minced
1 teaspoon chopped or crushed fresh or dried herbs

Place all ingredients in a shaker jar and blend thoroughly.

For RASPBERRY VINAIGRETTE, replace the wine vinegar with raspberry vinegar and omit the mustard and herbs. Blend as above.

INDEX